Learning More and Teaching Less

A Decade of Innovation in Self-instruction and Small Group Learning

Ilma M. Brewer

The Society for Research
into Higher Education
& NFER-NELSON

Published by SRHE & NFER-NELSON
At the University, Guildford, Surrey GU2 5XH

First published 1985
© Ilma M. Brewer
Oll 2703
ISBN 1 85059 003 6
Code 8938 021

378.17
Soc

129210

Typeset and Artwork by FD Graphics, Fleet, Hampshire.
Printed and bound in Great Britain
by Billing & Sons Limited, Worcester.

Foreword

Invitations to write forewords to books should be accepted only in one or other of two circumstances: either when some pundit wants to launch his protégé into the world of authorship, or when some disciple wants to put on record his gratitude to a master. Neither of these circumstances justifies this foreword. Why, then, did I agree to write it? It is because I want to put on record a confession. For many years I taught in universities. Like most academics I assumed that the only qualification I needed was expertise in the discipline I taught (which was biology). It did cross my mind that *how to teach* might be a discipline in its own right, but I never gave it much thought. I marked thousands of examination scripts without examining what the scripts could teach me about my capacity as a teacher and examiner.

Dr Brewer began her career, also in biology, with assumptions similar to mine. But, unlike most academics, she questioned the assumptions. This book is a record of her questioning. It led her, as an amateur, into the field of educational psychology. I am not competent to follow her there, but persons who are competent assure me that her book is a unique record of critical monitoring of a new learning technique. What I am competent to do after a lifetime in universities is to stress the need for university teachers to ask themselves the questions Dr Brewer has asked, and themselves to devise experiments in teaching and examining in order to get their own answers to these questions. I cannot imagine that any teacher could read this book without being challenged to examine his efficacy as a teacher and examiner.

Eric Ashby
1984

The Society for Research into Higher Education

The Society exists to encourage research and development in all aspects of higher education: highlighting both the importance of this and the needs of the research community. Its corporate members are universities, polytechnics, institutes of higher education, research institutions and professional and governmental bodies. Its individual members are teachers and researchers, administrators and students. Membership is worldwide, and the Society regards its international work as amongst its most important activities.

The Society discusses and comments on policy, organizes conferences and sponsors research. Under the imprint SRHE & NFER-NELSON it is a specialist publisher of research, with over thirty titles currently in print. It also publishes Studies in Higher Education (SHE) *(twice a year),* Research into Higher Education Abstracts *(three times a year),* Evaluation Newsletter (EN) *(twice a year),* International Newsletter (IN) *(twice a year) and a* Bulletin *(six times a year).*

The Society's committees, groups and local branches are run by members with limited help from a small secretariat and provide a forum for discussion and a platform for ideas. Some of the groups, at present the Teacher Education Study Group and the Staff Development Group, have their own subscriptions and organization, as do some local branches. The Governing Council, elected by members, comments on current issues and discusses policies with leading figures in politics and education. The Society organizes seminars on current research for officials of the DES and other ministries, and is in constant touch with officials of bodies such as the CNAA, NAB, CVCP, CDP, UGC and the British Council. The Society's annual conferences take up central themes, viz. Education for the Professions (1984, with the help and support of DTI, UNESCO and many professional bodies), Continuing Education (1985, organized in collaboration with Goldsmiths' College, the Open University and the University of Surrey, with advice from the DES and the CBI) and Standards (1986). Special studies are being commissioned. Joint conferences are held, viz. Cognitive Processes (1985, with the Cognitive Psychology Section of the BPS). Members receive free of charge the Society's Abstracts, SHE *(corporate members only), annual conference proceedings,* Bulletin *and* IN, *and may buy SRHE & NFER-NELSON books at discount. They may also obtain* EN *(published jointly with CRITE),* SHE *and certain other journals at discount.*

Further information from the Society for Research into Higher Education, At the University, Guildford GU2 5XH, UK.

Preface

This book is remarkable in two respects. It is a compressed record of ten years of research in university teaching, and the teaching involved the combination of individual and peer-group work. Circumstances of lifestyle, of course, made Dr Brewer's experience possible. She came back to university teaching after a period of child-rearing to an environment pregnant with the promises of educational technology, resonating with such names as Bloom and Postlethwait. Small group teaching was beginning to flourish. Australia was generous with sabbatical leave, and she travelled a lot. Her mind was free to adopt these innovations and to adapt them to the scientific conventions of her earlier teaching experience of botany. She set up a laboratory based on audio-visual technology (which came to be known locally as The Brewery) in which individuals learnt the substance of plant anatomy. Small group teaching was an integral part of her original package. But in this highly visual subject, full exploitation of the advantages of peer-group interaction was not realized until she was able to introduce projected slides for problem-based discussion.

Small group teaching recognizes that man is essentially a social animal, and a talking one, and that individual learning from highly organized self-instruction can be helped by freer, less organized discussion in peer groups. It provides a social situation which not only improves possibilities of feedback, but also cashes in on the strong learning potentialities of expressive behaviour. We all know how much more difficult it is to speak a foreign language than it is to understand it!

When reading the book it is important to keep in mind that Dr Brewer was primarily interested in improving teaching and learning, and not in researching in education. Nevertheless, she made records of the procedures and their effects as meticulous as those she had made as a researcher in plant ecology. The book is thus a natural history of a series of innovations made in educational practice. The proof of her pudding is not in a one-off comparison of highly selected and rigorously treated experimental and control groups. It is in the comparison of before-and-after populations studied in natural conditions, and made by an observer wary of the many other factors that inevitably vary besides the intended innovation.

I hope that the publication of this book will encourage other teachers to follow the author's example. The techniques used are by no means limited to plant anatomy, or to botany: any subject with a high visual content could clearly be handled in a very similar manner. Indeed, it could well be argued that Dr Brewer's combination of self-instruction with problem-based group discussion could serve as a prototype for work in many subject areas. But to translate such an approach into action requires courage and persistence and I for one am grateful to Dr Brewer for carrying through so far-reaching a project and for undertaking the long effort of presenting it to a wider audience.

M.L.J. Abercrombie
1984

Contents

Acknowledgements

This book records an experiment in higher education designed and monitored by myself over ten years, from 1969 to 1978. The experiment could not have been done without a great deal of help. It is a pleasure, therefore, to begin the record with some acknowledgements.

I am deeply indebted to Eric Ashby (professor of botany in the University of Sydney from 1938-46) for constant support, and in particular for his advice and generous editorial assistance with the various drafts of the MS.

Many other people have helped me in different ways, but I first acknowledge the generosity of Jane Abercrombie in reading and commenting on the entire penultimate draft of the MS, and giving encouragement during the course of the project. Her death is deeply mourned. To Sam Postlethwait and the late Fred Katz I record my thanks for their continued interest and stimulating discussions throughout the development of the study.

I am indebted also to David Tomlinson, co-author of two published papers, for allowing our joint work to be incorporated in this book, and for his continued help with statistical analysis of data. We both record our thanks to Don Spearitt for advice on statistical methods, and to the Education Research and Development Committee of the Australian Department of Education and Science (ERDC) for supporting Dr Tomlinson as a senior research assistant from 1976-78 in our research project on learning profiles of individual students. I am grateful for permission from the journals concerned to incorporate excerpts from five published papers (Brewer 1974, 1977, 1979 and Brewer and Tomlinson 1981 a, b).

Without the support of the University of Sydney and my colleagues in the School of Biological Sciences, this experiment could not have been done. In 1968 the University of Sydney made a special grant to set up a learning centre in the Botany Building.

With perhaps some tremor of initial trepidation, the School of Biological Sciences gave me a free hand to design a course of instruction which was not only a departure from traditional methods, but also required departmental adjustments to be made to the incompatible university timetables.

Since my retirement at the end of 1978, Michael Blunt, professor of anatomy in the University of Sydney, has kindly provided me – as an honorary research affiliate – with accommodation and the use of departmental facilities.

It is a pleasure to acknowledge the help from technical staff: to June Jeffrey (biology) for the graphic illustrations; to Bert Lester (biology) and Clive Jeffrey (anatomy) for their reproduction; to Bert Lester for all the photographs and photomicrographs which are still used in the learning centre and in the study guide; jointly to Bert Lester and Jim Fairburn for the production − over a period of years − of most of the three hundred colour-slide transparencies (photomicrographs of plant sections) currently in use for group discussions.

I am grateful to the tutors and students who have helped to collect data used for evaluation, and especially to students from 1976 to 1978, who co-operated in the tiresome task of filling in questionnaires used for the project on individual learning profiles.

Finally I would like to express my gratitude and thanks to Gerald Collier (Publications Committee, Society for Research into Higher Education) for his invaluable and detailed suggestions for reshaping the final draft of the monograph.

1 Learning More and Teaching Less

INTRODUCTION

Three centuries ago Comenius wrote that his object was 'to seek and find a method by which the teachers teach less and the learners learn more' (Comenius 1896). University teachers involved in educational reform are still taking part in his search. Many innovations have been tried but few of them have been critically assessed over the long term, to find out what the results really are. The work reported here is a case history of ten years of innovation and adaptation, by one teacher, seeking what Comenius sought and – this is the most important feature – assessing by quantitative techniques the efficacy of the innovations. Short-term studies of this kind are to be found in the technical journals on education, but few university teachers in subjects other than education read these journals.

This book is addressed primarily to teachers who want to know whether these new methods of teaching can be applied in their own work, and if so, how they can monitor the innovations. Nevertheless, the book has two functions for two different kinds of readers: a handbook for practitioners and an advocate's case for reform of teaching techniques. Perhaps also the professionals may see some of the principles of educational technology reflected here in a way which would motivate others to experiment with educational reform in their own fields.

Some Deficiencies of Contemporary Higher Education

The Hale report (1964) into tertiary education in Britain stated that 'an implicit aim of higher education is to encourage students to think for themselves'. While lip-service is paid to this belief amongst university teachers, many of them, nevertheless, are content to teach and test in a style which lays stress less upon thinking than upon giving information. A surprisingly high proportion of factual recall items are among questions in many final examinations (McGuire 1963; Beard 1972). In anticipation of this, students become adept at last-minute 'cramming'. Much of the information tested in examination involves learning by rote material readily available in textbooks; the process of memorizing it is often of little subsequent value. To know facts is obviously essential for any discipline but it is not the function of tertiary education to lay undue emphasis on this aspect at the expense of other cognitive skills which may prove more useful. Cognitive skills are, however, more difficult to test in examinations, and this

1

may well be one reason why questions calling for application, analysis, synthesis and evaluation (Bloom 1956) are not more commonly set.

The prevalence among students of dependence on formal instruction is perhaps nothing more than a reflection on the reluctance of many of their teachers to offer an alternative. When alternative methods of instruction are offered, there is usually no lack-of student volunteers. A current example at the University of Sydney (personal communication, Blunt 1983) was the call for a maximum of fifty volunteers (from about 250 enrolled) to study the course on medical anatomy (five terms across the second and third years) by the Keller Plan (Keller 1968). This requires independent, self-paced study of self-instructional materials, each unit of which is tested for mastery; tutorial reinforcement is given when required. More than the required number of students volunteered for the Keller-based course, even though the current — and very effective — method of teaching anatomy was not traditional (lectures and dissection of the whole body), but included, in addition to some lectures, self-instruction with museum and prosected specimens, small group discussions and optional dissection (Blunt 1979).

A recognized deficiency of contemporary education is the difficulty in developing habits of independent judgement in students, particularly if instruction is in large groups. 'Buzz' sessions in lectures may alleviate the difficulty: the lecturer invites the class to discuss briefly — in groups of 2-6 — particular ideas, issues or problems. Peer learning and discussion in small groups can be effective in boosting self-confidence and self-image, necessary for some students in developing habits of independent judgement. One of the most successful techniques used in peer-group learning is the syndicate method (Collier 1983). 'In a syndicate-based course, the class is divided into syndicates of 4-8 students and the bulk of the work consists of a series of assignments carried out on a co-operative basis by the syndicates acting as teams, for much of the time in the absence of the teacher. ... The heart of the technique is the intensive debate within the syndicates.' The syndicate-based work may either constitute the whole course or a component designed to develop particular higher order skills (Collier 1980).

The different techniques used by proponents of group work have been reviewed by Abercrombie (1979), who pioneered (1960) the use of 'free' or 'associative' group discussion for training in observation and reasoning, with students controlling the direction of the discussion. She writes (1978) that 'the distinctive contribution that small group teaching can make to education is in encouraging students to become more autonomous as learners.' If these and similar techniques for involving students in the learning process, eg peer tutoring (Goldschmid 1976), were used more frequently, students who presently lack commitment in their approach to academic study may find learning more stimulating and relevant.

Teachers in tertiary education believe — though not everyone is willing to act on the belief - in the need to place emphasis on intellectual skills and problem-solving strategies, rather than on presently known facts. But the main criterion for appointments to teaching posts in universities is ability to do research, rather than to teach. Hence lecturers are not likely to be interested in educational innovation; they are not familiar with the potential of fresh teaching techniques. It is no wonder that traditional methods survive: we tend to teach as we were taught.

How then can students be encouraged to develop higher order skills, to think for themselves, and to adopt a critical approach to learning? The challenge should be presented by those who teach them. The way in which they study, and the learning skills acquired in the process, are dictated by the way they are tested. As expressed so succinctly by Bruner (1961), 'It matters not *what* we have learned. What we can *do* with what we have learned; this is the issue... let us not judge our students simply on *what* they know.... Rather, let them be judged on what they can generate from what they know — how well they can leap the barrier from learning to thinking.'

THE PROJECT

For many decades, plant anatomy — like other branches of natural science — was taught at Sydney University in the traditional style, by lectures and laboratory classes. I inherited this course in 1965, and continued the traditional style of instruction until 1968. In 1969, I began to develop a technique of self-instruction, using audiotapes with a variety of audio-visual and printed media.

As with most innovations, the change was made partly in response to learners' needs for a more stimulating presentation of this highly factual subject — ideally suited to audio-visual instruction — and to a growing dissatisfaction on my part with the conventional teaching of some 120 students by two lectures and two 6-hour laboratory classes a week (necessitated by a maximum capacity of sixty in the laboratory).

Between 1965 and 1968, while I was teaching the course in the traditional style, I spent a lot of time preparing visual aids for lectures, revising the curriculum, and producing a comprehensive laboratory manual for students, to encourage independent work. The results were unrewarding. The catalyst for change was a meeting with Professor S. N. Postlethwait in Sydney in 1968 and, shortly after, a visit to Purdue University, the scene — in the early sixties — of his fresh approach to learning by the audio-tutorial (A-T) system (Postlethwait et al. 1969). Late in 1968 the University of Sydney agreed to set up, in the Botany building, a self-instructional learning centre, modelled on Postlethwait's A-T system. By February 1969 the Botany Library (in disuse following the merger of several departmental libraries) had been transformed into a learning centre with twenty-four carrels and a large display area for demonstrations. Each carrel had a tape recorder with independent listening facilities for audiotapes; the only other items of 'hardware' in the centre were two units for daylight viewing of tape-slides.

Since 1969 the material to be learnt has been assembled in 'packages' called *modules*, which combine, in one study session lasting a week, investigation of laboratory material with theoretical aspects of the subject. Students are able to set their own times and pace of learning. To this extent it is modelled on Postlethwait's A-T system. Self-instruction is complemented by discussion between tutors and students each week in small groups, to probe into the implications of the module studied during the previous week.

When the centre opened, in March 1969, for 119 second-year science and agriculture students, only three modules of the nine required for the course were complete: the rest were in various stages of draft. It was like putting a play on the stage before the last scene had been written. In the event, but only after some breathless scrambles to meet deadlines each week, the modules were all ready in time.

Although it could not be recommended as a pattern to be followed, there was one definite advantage in completing the production of modules while the course was running. By spending a great deal of time in the learning centre talking to students, and by using student feedback from weekly questionnaires, it was possible to avoid many of the mistakes made initially by programmers who prepare a whole course before using it in the classroom.

During the next few years, I continued to improve the content and presentation of modules. Occasionally, colleagues were co-opted as critics of scripts for audiotapes and tape-slides, but the initial programming of the course was my responsibility. The audiotapes were regularly revised and re-recorded for the first five years; and with minor alterations to some during 1975-1978, they have been used subsequently without change.

Small groups of 8-10 students, meeting regularly each week with a tutor, to discuss the content of the module studied the previous week, have always been an essential part of the course, but for the first three years the scope of discussions was restricted by the absence of suitable facilities for providing visual examples. In 1972, by converting an adjoining room into a seminar room, and installing two slide projectors on one wall, it became feasible to use the whole of the opposite wall as a large screen for colour-slide transparencies of plant sections. Group members, with seating arranged in a U-shape, were then able to view and discuss the large images of plant sections that had previously been examined by microscopic study in the learning centre. In this way their powers of *comprehension, recall* and *recognition* could be tested. By using previously unseen material, the groups could then practise the *application* of principles and concepts learned in module study. The response from students now became much more lively. Year by year the techniques were refined in such a way as to stimulate critical discussion and to introduce concepts of higher order skills such as *analysis, synthesis* and *evaluation* in solving simple anatomical problems.

A printed question paper was associated with this visual presentation; in tandem paper and presentation provided the framework for peer discussion. Some questions required individual written answers prior to discussion; these were scored for continuing assessment.

Concurrently with changes in the degree of sophistication of the group work, changes were made in the final examination to assess higher order skills; students were required to solve complex problems for which they had received no direct instruction in the group sessions. Over the 10-year period discussed in this book the level of difficulty was raised by increasing the percentage marks awarded to problem questions (from 26% in 1971 to 80% in 1978) and by reducing the proportion of marks for questions requiring merely recognition or recall of knowledge, then in 1973 by omitting these recall questions altogether. Annual adjustments to proportions of the other question type (application) preserved the 100% constitution of the examination.

By 1974 it had become evident that students varied widely in their responses to teaching by these techniques, which prompted an inquiry into the *learning profiles* of individual students. The profiles are composed from curves depicting the attainment of individual students, measured in weekly assessment tests given during group sessions. The assessment tests measured performance in four capacities, based on what are known as Bloom's (1956) criteria, viz. the capacity to recall and recognize, the capacity to comprehend, the capacity to apply information, and the capacity to use these and other higher order skills in the solution of short-chain problems. Learning curves for each of these four capacities were obtained for each of about 300 students during the four years of the study, from 1975 to 1978.

Personal attributes (from tests administered during the course — see Appendix A) such as anxiety-levels, learning preferences, field dependence/ independence (a visual skill), together with age, sex, general ability (from previous academic performance), interest in the course, motivation and reactions to various aspects of the teaching method (from questionnaires about the course) were determined for each student and have added other variables to the individual learning profiles of students.

I therefore had all the necessary raw material for both objective and subjective evaluation of the efficacy of the teaching method (defined p. 7) as a tool for learning.

EVALUATION

When I made the changeover from traditional teaching in 1969, no attempt was made to monitor the change in a rigorous way. There were no experimental and control groups; all students used the new method of self-instruction.

Throughout the period of study, records were kept (see Appendix A: Records and Tests) of the responses of students to questionnaires about the course, their scores in weekly assessments in the groups, and in final examination, and all their examination scripts. This allowed retrospective analysis of changes in performance across years. Meticulous records were also kept of all materials used in modules and in groups, so that the possible effect on performance of changes made to media used in group discussions or in self-instruction could also be analysed.

Based on these records, I was able to evaluate the teaching techniques over the ten years 1969-78, and the performance of students by two methods of assessment. The overall performance of students in final examination, and specifically their improvement of performance in complex problem-solving questions was evaluated over years in relation to the difficulty of the examination, changes made to media, especially those used in group discussions, and other variables.

To speak of 'mastery' of the course is somewhat pretentious. But there has to be some arbitrary measure of success, and the measure I adopted was a score of 80%. It would, course, be unrealistic to expect every student to reach this level; my aim was to develop a technique which would increase the proportion of students who mastered the course (in this sense) over the proportion one would expect anyway for a course taught by traditional techniques. It was rewarding to record the gradual increase in numbers of students achieving mastery in weekly tests and final examination, and the accompanying decrease in the proportion of students failing.

The value of the teaching method rests on hard evidence that in certain respects it is a better tool for learning than the traditional method. This has been demonstrated for the cohorts from 1975 to 1978 by an improvement in test-scores across the weekly tests during the course, with the mean score increasing by approximately 10% within each cohort. This improvement was not uniform; it was accomplished by approximately 80 per cent of the sample of about 300 students over the four years. Some kinds of students appeared to benefit more than others, but not all of these were able to carry the improvement over into the final examination. Most of those whose performance in the weekly tests was consistently high – and therefore did not appear to improve – exceeded expectations by their superior examination performance.

Using the data from records of individual performance in the different cognitive categories of tests over weeks, the individual responses – learning profiles – of some 300 students in the 1975-78 cohorts were graphed. Four major patterns of response emerged, indicating different styles of intellectual development. These were called *profile types*. From the profile types it was possible to make some predictions about performance in final examination, although this examination was predominantly one to test capacity to solve long-chain, multi-step problems, for which there had been no specific preparation in the group discussions. Support for the validity of these profile types comes from their distribution within the frequency distribution of examination scores, and from the diversity in occurrence of other attributes and variables between profile types.

An overall summary of this ten-year study can be put into one sentence: as the teaching method was refined, more students mastered the subject and fewer failed. To confirm that the refinements created the better performance it was necessary to examine other possible causes, eg that in later years students spent more time on self-instruction than they had in earlier years. Fortunately, from records of the time spent on modules (Appendix A: Records and Tests) it was possible to demonstrate that this was not the reason for the success of the technique.

Statistical analysis of results from final examination and continuing assessment gives objective information about the efficacy of the method. But it is important to have some qualitative impression of whether or not students like to be taught – or to learn – this way. Accordingly, students were asked to fill in questionnaires (and over 98 per cent of each cohort co-operated), asking them what they thought of the course and how they regarded specific aspects of it. Apart from their consistent endorsement of the overall method, perhaps the most interesting information elicited from questionnaires is their perception of how various teaching techniques used in the groups have aided their own learning.

Of course I have also talked informally to students, tutors, former students, and visitors to the learning centre. It is well known that there is a certain attraction about novelty itself – which might elicit appreciation – and that face-to-face conversations often evoke opinions designed to 'please the teacher'. Nevertheless, the very high proportion of favourable subjective impressions I have received from most students over the period of the study seems to be endorsed by the results of the questionnaires reported in Chapter 8.

Naturally students forget some of what they have learnt after they finish the course. Decisive information is not available about the persistence of concepts and facts that students learn, though this has been studied at various time intervals for a small sample and is briefly discussed in Appendix

B: Attrition. In any case, persistence depends on the use made afterwards of the information; it was A. N. Whitehead who wrote that 'knowledge keeps no better than fish'.

I emphasize the need to add a subjective dimension to the objective data resting on assessment by weekly tests and final examination, because this book would leave a false impression if it were thought that some 1000 students have been treated as experimental guinea pigs in order to satisfy my enthusiasm for a novel style of education. My purpose was to make into a challenging adventure a subject which can be very tedious when badly taught, and in no way to sacrifice its intellectual rigour. Perhaps the best testimony to the acceptability in the department of the course is that it has survived virtually unchanged since I retired from teaching at the end of 1978.

SIMIG: THE ACRONYM DEFINED

The model for the experiment in Sydney was Postlethwait's (1969) audio-tutorial (A-T) approach, developed for 'freshman' courses in botany and biology. But as the intellectual demands made upon the students increased and the style of the group discussions changed, the method diverged from the A-T model. The interaction of students with one another during the discussions brought a more analytical approach toward the material. Comprehension, recall, and recognition — still important, of course — became the baseline for more sophisticated reasoning about the material. So much so, that I felt myself justified in adding still one more acronym to the constellation already circulating in this field: Self-Instruction by Modules was being followed by Interaction among Groups during discussion, justifying (I trust) the creation of the acronym SIMIG for the innovation developed over the ten years in Sydney.

The type of discussion group used in SIMIG has not been described in the literature, but Abercrombie (1960, 1970) has greatly influenced the later stages of my approach to group work, in particular by her emphasis on the tutor's style in facilitating peer interaction and in the techniques devised originally (1960) to aid development of the capacity to make scientific judgements.

The SIMIG method thus combines two strategies which in the last two decades have attracted considerable interest in educational innovation, viz. self-instruction done independently without a teacher, and learning by discussion in small groups.

In addition, the SIMIG method has involved the systematic use of audio-visual media in the presentation of material both for independent self-instruction and for group discussion. To this has been added a procedure for assessment designed specifically to test the development of higher order skills, over and above the recall of information.

PLAN OF THIS BOOK

Ten years of trial and error went into designing the new educational strategy described in this book. It cannot be described with the smooth rationality of a planned experiment in educational psychology, for it was not an experiment: it was a by-product of practical experience. My prime consideration was to teach some 120 students each year in the rudiments of plant anatomy;

the niceties of experimental method had to be subservient to this end. As new challenges arose I had to make new responses. It is the processes as much as the end results which are likely to be of interest.

The following outline of each chapter will help to guide the reader through the inevitable detail of the study.

Chapter 2 This chapter outlines the procedures for self-instruction: the production of units or modules of study; the provision of a study guide for each student; and the use of audio-visual techniques for the presentation of the academic material. Illustrative excerpts are given (in the notes at the end of the chapter) from one module in the study guide and an audiotape. Distinctive features of self-instruction are contrasted briefly with traditional methods of instruction.

Chapter 3 An account is given of the techniques used in group discussions; the evolution of ways of presenting visual material, and the tutor's role in facilitating the discussion to place greater emphasis on higher order cognitive skills. Short excerpts are given from transcripts of discussion in the second and ninth weeks of the course. A summary is given of how the combination of self-instruction and group discussion here adopted in the SIMIG method fulfils conditions for effective learning.

Chapter 4 An account is given of the way in which the techniques of assessment were evolved in order to assess students' academic progress in accordance with university requirements, and at the same time to test how far the experimental techniques were in fact succeeding in developing higher order intellectual skills. Weekly tests were given in conjunction with the group discussions (the continuing assessment discussed in Chapter 5) and a final examination at the end of the term (the summative assessment). Both these involved a gradually increasing emphasis on problems calling for higher order skills. An example of a problem question from a final examination is given. There follows a detailed analysis of the results of the final examination for the 10 years 1969-78, supported by statistical evidence (given in the notes at the end of the chapter). The controversial question is raised as to whether examination scores should of necessity conform to a normal distribution.

Chapter 5 This chapter outlines how the changes (described in Chapter 3) made in the group discussions to the quality and quantity of the media that was being used increased their degree of sophistication, and shows what influence this had on examination scores, particularly of problem questions – exemplified by a critical 'experiment' (one of the few I deliberately devised).

It is evident from Chapters 4 and 5 that the SIMIG method did indeed significantly increase mastery and decrease failure rates in the cohorts of students whose scores were analysed.

Chapter 6 I present and discuss the scores for the weekly tests for cohorts from 1975-78. These fall into some interesting combinations of frequency distributions: nearly normal in the early weeks of the term and becoming skewed toward better performance as students became adapted to the intellectual demands made upon them in the group discussions. The influence of time spent in module study on weekly test scores is analysed, and there is a brief discussion of some aspects of peer learning in SIMIG groups.

Chapter 7 The conclusion from Chapters 4 and 5 – that the SIMIG method increases mastery and decreases failure rate – is examined from a different point of view, namely how do different kinds of students (as determined from their examination scores at entry to and in the first year at university) respond to different levels of sophistication in the examination questions set in the SIMIG course. It is established that students with different 'learning profiles' perform differently.

Chapter 8 Statistical data alone are insufficient to assess the value of an innovation in teaching; it is essential also to know what attitude the students themselves take towards the innovation. Accordingly, each year, questionnaires were circulated to students who had taken the course. About one thousand replied; their responses are analysed in this chapter.

Chapter 9 Any new strategy for teaching and learning must be cost-effective: an analysis of costs of SIMIG compared with traditional methods is presented. (Application of SIMIG to other disciplines is also discussed.)

Chapter 10 An account is given of the main innovations made by others to which I am indebted – self-instruction by the audio-tutorial method, group discussion techniques, self-pacing and mastery learning – and I offer my own reflections on the results of the ten-year study.

For the general reader, or the reader interested primarily in the analysis of the efficacy of the SIMIG technique, the practical details of Chapters 2 and 3 may be of less interest than to protagonists of self-instruction or small group learning. But the reader should be warned that some of the conclusions about the efficacy of the course arise from the annual adjustments made in the content of the group discussions (Chapter 3).

2 Tools for Learning: 1 Self-instruction by Modules

This chapter summarizes general features of the method of self-instruction, components of modules, and the introduction of students to the teaching techniques. Descriptions are given of how students use modules in the learning centre, and of the four types of media and the rationale for their use. The advantages of this method of self-instruction are contrasted briefly with conventional methods of teaching practical science subjects. Reference notes, in the appendix to the chapter, include excerpts from an audiotape script, guidelines used in its preparation, and two pages from the study guide.

THE METHOD

Self-instruction, based on Postlethwait's (1969) audio-tutorial method, takes place in a multi-media learning centre. Twenty-four carrels (booths) for independent study are equipped with the software especially prepared for the course (audiotapes and photomicrographs of plant sections) and the appropriate hardware (cassette tape-decks and headsets). Students bring their own study guides — another essential item of software; they may also bring a recommended textbook. All the materials used in a conventional plant anatomy course are also in the carrels (prepared slides for use with microscopes, fresh specimens for hand-cut sections, and staining reagents).

During the nine weeks of the course there are eight modules (units of self-instruction), and one major project — equivalent to a module. Modules are presented in succession, one at a time for one week only; consequently, self-pacing has to be fitted into one week.

The learning centre is open all day; students may choose their own study times: some prefer to take one time block to complete a module study; others make several visits during the week. One demonstrator is either present or 'on call'.

In the display areas of the learning centre, various exhibits, demonstrations, literature, and audio-visual programmes complement or supplement carrel study. These are the so-called 'enrichment materials'.

MODULES

Every module has four components: the audiotape used in conjunction with the study guide, the carrel materials and the 'enrichment' materials.

The *audiotape* guides the learner through the study session for each module. The main purpose of the tape is to integrate theoretical aspects (as in lectures) with individual investigations by the student (as in a laboratory). The average listening time for audiotapes is forty-five minutes, but the frequent and obligatory interruptions for examination of plant materials both within the carrel and elsewhere in the centre result in an average study time for each module of about five hours.

An audiotape index correlates the approximate number on the cassette tape-counter with the relevant section in the study guide. This facilitates 'tape-search' for replay of particular sections.

Audiotapes are available for overnight or weekend loan. There are not many requests for them, as it is more effective and convenient to complete the module in the learning centre with the relevant material at hand.

The *study guide* is an essential companion to self-instruction; it complements all the audiotapes for the course; neither study guide nor audiotape alone is sufficient. It provides – in about thirty pages for each of the eight modules – a comprehensive record of the content of carrel study, presented in strict sequence with the audiotape. It fulfils several purposes, presenting for each module the following:

- Index of contents and figures, materials supplied in the carrels, and demonstrations.
- Introductory statement of the general instructional and specific objectives (Mager 1962), followed by a list of the associated learning activities.
- Summaries of each section of the tapescript with relevant tables, graphs, and illustrations.
- Directions for practical work.
- Reproductions of some of the annotated photomicrographs of plant sections provided in the carrels.
- Quizzes for self-assessment at appropriate intervals, to test comprehension rather than recall of facts.
- References, and suggested answers to self-quizzes.

Carrel materials for plant anatomy are essentially microscope slides of plant sections for use with a microscope. Fresh specimens are used for hand-cut sections, but most examinations are made using prepared, permanently-stained slides. For each module the twenty-four boxes of prepared slides in carrels are almost identical. Corresponding sets of labelled photomicrographs (black and white, 25 x 20 cms) made from these slides assist students in the microscopic identification of tissues.

A revision carrel, with the audiotape, box of slides and photomicrographs of the module studied the previous week, allows students who have been absent to catch up. For the 'revision' week preceding final examinations these three items for the eight modules are set up in triplicate in the twenty-four carrels, and all sixteen tape-slides (see below) are available for replay.

Enrichment materials in the display area of the learning centre amplify carrel study; they include:

- Demonstration slides (under microscopes), with annotated photomicrographs on the wall.
- Fresh specimens of plants used in permanent microscope slides, and extra material for optional sections.

- Plant exhibits illustrating diversity in form of the plant organ examined in the module.
- Relevant literature, including reference textbooks and reprints of research papers – this brings the library into the learning centre.
- Two tape-slides for each module: one is a summary of the most important anatomical concepts and features in the module – useful for review or revision; the second adds background interest and provides another dimension to a highly factual subject in which instruction is essentially by microscopic study.

INTRODUCING STUDENTS TO THE METHOD

Any teaching method which departs from the familiar traditional pattern so entrenched in universities is liable to be a perplexing experience for at least some students. To lessen this effect, I planned an introductory meeting which, for this course, was the first and last time the whole class met together. The first scheduled lecture time-slot was an opportunity for this introductory session.

Students were given several hand-outs, including course outlines for the whole year, details of the anatomy course, and assessment measures. A tape-slide on the teaching method occupied the next twenty minutes and depicted students arriving at the centre, checking in, and becoming involved in self-directed activities in the learning centre and finally in the group discussions. So, on their first visit, students were already familiar with the procedures to be followed in the learning centre.

USING MODULES FOR SELF-INSTRUCTION

The modules present all the essential information and material, but it is the student who must assume responsibility for his* own learning. With *self-pacing*, the individual decides how much time he needs – or is willing to spend – on each module. This varies widely (three to eight hours), but time spent is not necessarily reflected by performance in assessment tests (see Chapters 4, 6).

In the carrel, the student turns on the tape, listens to the introduction and is referred to the relevant page in his study guide, where the objectives for the module are listed. It is emphasis placed on clear statements of the *general and specific objectives* that draws attention to the main aspects to be covered, and ensures that the learner does not get lost in less important details. At the end of the first few audiotapes the student is reminded to check the list of objectives, and asked to decide whether he has achieved them: an important decision, as in the following week group discussions and test items are based on these objectives.

The audiotape involves the learner at all stages of presentation: he is not a passive recipient of information but is guided by the tape through a comprehensive series of investigations to allow him to achieve the stated objectives. The tape is structured to integrate *facts and concepts with practical examples*; listening periods alternate with independent examinations; the

---

*I have had to decide how to refer to the sex of a student throughout this book. To write 'he or she', 'him or her', dozens of times, seems pedantic. I have therefore adopted the convention that the word 'student' is masculine, even though some 40 per cent of students – including many of the brightest – are female.

student frequently has to stop the tape to investigate material either inside or outside the carrel. Even during listening periods — usually less than five minutes — it is possible to involve the learner by asking him to look at a relevant figure, table or graph in the study guide, or to pick up a carrel specimen — with a pause in the tape while the item is located (this chapter, Note 1).

In the carrel, study is based on examination of permanent microscope slides (stained with specific colour dyes), all numbered for easy cross reference to study guide and audiotape index. Students also cut, stain and examine sections prepared from fresh material in the carrel; they may also conduct simple experiments. The sets of labelled *photomicrographs* of plant sections of some — but not all — permanent slides, allow students to interpret anatomical details without help from a demonstrator — although such help is readily available if required. With sections not illustrated by photomicrographs, students have to apply knowledge gained from previous examples. In this way inquiry, discovery and confidence are fostered, and autonomous learning is encouraged.

At all times it is the student who controls the rate of presentation of material. Any part of the tape can be reversed and replayed; an advantage to the slow learner who can, unobtrusively and without stress, use this facility as often as required. For revision, tape search for particular sections is expedited by reference to the *tape index* and the corresponding number on the tape-counter, in conjunction with the fast forward/reverse controls. The whole module can be revised either by replaying the audiotape without repeating the associated activities, or by reading the study guide. For many students, these facilities for study vastly increase comprehension. They are adaptations, impossible in the lecture/laboratory method, to the different learning rates of different students.

The study guide is the student's private workbook, so advice to use the spaces for written answers to self-quizzes is almost always followed; immediate *feedback* is provided by suggested answers in the appendix to each module. Students may also discuss their answers or their problems with the demonstrator or with their peers.

The demonstrator does not approach students uninvited, but by occasionally walking around the carrels, he or she may be seen to be available and interested to help if required.

Although the atmosphere in the learning centre is one of quiet concentration, it would be misleading to give the impression that students are isolated, rather than private, in their individual carrels, for they often leave them to consult one another, exchange hand-cut sections or to look at demonstrations which cannot be included in the carrels.

Use of the demonstrations and exhibits and so on in the display areas of the learning centre is at the students' discretion, but the appropriate time to examine particular items is indicated by the audiotape or study guide. For example, it is suggested that the best time for viewing the anatomy tape-slide (module summary) is on completion of carrel study.

To encourage *autonomy*, some of the modules incorporate minor independent investigations which may be submitted for comment. There is no module in the seventh week: students are assigned (individually) a major anatomical *project*. Reference books are available but no other help is given.

Reports are marked and returned at the following group session, when each student also gives a short oral report to his own group, all of whom have investigated a different plant.

It is evident that, to master each module, the student has to make *effective use of aural, visual and printed media*, both in the carrels and in the demonstration areas of the learning centre.

MEDIA IN SELF-INSTRUCTIONAL MODULES
The selection and use of the appropriate media for presenting material, and the quality of this *software* determines the efficacy of modules as tools for learning.

Irrespective of the quality of the software, recurring technical faults and/or a high breakdown rate of equipment detract from any presentation: the *hardware* should be reliable, not necessarily expensive. In the learning centre, the high quality of the tapes and tape recorders in the carrels (open-reel 1969-76, cassettes from 1977) has ensured clarity of reproduction and a high performance record. With the tape-slide equipment, features which ensure ease of viewing include electronic pulsing units for automatic and inaudible slide change, rear screen projection for daylight viewing, and multiple headphone outlets to accommodate viewing by one to four students.

Four types of media, and the rationale for their use in this course are considered: audiotapes (aural), study guide (printed and visual), photo-micrographs (visual), and tape-slides (audio-visual).

Audiotapes
Audiotapes are used to simulate a one to one relationship between teacher and student. The style of recorded speech to be aimed at is the informal conversation which would be used in a tutorial, with teacher and student sitting down together; the term audio-tutorial (A-T) is derived from this concept.

The audiotape is not based exclusively on what Bruner (1961) called expository or discovery learning; it is a balance between the two which may be described as a form of *guided discovery*. Structuring of the audiotape provides a medium which is most suitable for concept learning. Emphasis is placed on diagnostic features which both discriminate and define concepts. The tape frequently guides and occasionally prompts the student as he identifies the concepts essential for understanding each module. It is possible to construct the audiotape to invoke new stimuli, give specific and defining examples, provide reinforcement and varied repetition of the main ideas, and encourage generalizations necessary for transfer of learning.

The diversity of activities suggested requires almost continual overt responses, with the student himself controlling the rate at which the material is presented. Branch investigations may be presented so the student is free to wander into areas of interest and then 'pick up the threads' by returning to the audiotape.

All master tapes for this course have been revised and recorded many times. Especially in the initial productions, comments from staff and students gave rise to useful suggestions; when several students asked the same question in the learning centre it was a sign that a particular section of the tapescript required clarification. The extent to which revision and refinement have been successful can be judged by student responses to questionnaires about the course. The first audiotapes (a novel experience) were enthusiastically received; this enthusiasm did not diminish with increasing sophistication of presentation and content: eg in 1976 (the eighth year of the SIMIG course) nine out of ten of the class (n = 71) were favourably impressed with the integration of theory and practical work (Table 21, item 2).

For the first five years, audiotapes were recorded using only one voice; in 1974 the addition of another voice (making one of each sex) gave a variety which the students liked. Even though listening periods are short, a change in voice timbre prevents monotony and adds interest. The detailed planning of audiotapes is of the greatest importance. Not surprisingly, preparation of an audioscript is time-consuming (approximately forty hours for a 45-minute tape). An entirely different technique is required compared with writing a lecture or a laboratory manual. Over the course of time I formulated a set of guidelines for the preparation of audiotapes. An excerpt from the introduction to one audiotape is given here to illustrate these guidelines (this chapter, Notes 1 and 2).

Study Guide
As indicated previously, the study guide is an essential companion to the equipment for self-instruction. The specification of important objectives in the study guide may act as advance organizers, especially when coupled with preliminary instructions on the audiotape. The different types of feedback both from audiotape and from self-quizzes in the study guide – and suggested responses – allow the learner to monitor his performance at various stages of self-instruction.

The study guide for the SIMIG course differs in some respects from typical A-T guides, where the student is usually required to summarize sections of the audiotape. With the plant anatomy course, involving five hours of concentrated work, I decided that the study guide should be a complete take-away package, providing an accurate summary of each module. Sections of the tape, especially information not readily available in textbooks, or complicated theoretical aspects, are printed in full. Students (especially those of anxious temperament) might otherwise be tempted to transcibe sections of the audiotape; indeed I observed as much in the initial years, before the printed study guide was provided. Of course this activity is similar to getting a set of notes from lectures. Relieved of this need, students can devote their time in the learning centre to looking at the material and comprehending the concepts involved.

In the current (1977) edition there are 280 pages, 60 reproductions of photomicrographs, and 75 figures for eight modules (this chapter, Note 3). After two years with xeroxed notes, a study guide was printed in 1971, with three revisions in succeeding years. In the second edition (1975), a project was substituted for one of the nine modules; four modules were reorganized into three; the remaining five were recast and expanded. These changes may have contributed to improvement in performance, either in final examination or in response to weekly test items. Revisions of the study guide necessarily involve revision and re-recording of relevant audiotapes, since they are complementary and for clarity must be strictly in sequence.

For each module in the study guide, there is an index of content, a list of materials provided, and lists of objectives and learning activities (this chapter, Note 4). Other characteristic features are illustrated here in two pages from the first module (Note 5).

Photomicrographs

Annotated black and white photomicrographs (approximately twenty per module) were chosen as the most appropriate augmentation to the microscopic study of plant sections. Photomicrographs (made from the same slides used by students) enable students to identify all tissues without help from the teacher. There is accordingly no need for the demonstrator to spend time on that traditional task in the conventional laboratory course on plant anatomy: using an ocular pointer over and over again to identify some tissue to one student after another. In questionnaires about the course, the ratings given to the question 'How much have you relied on demonstrator help in interpreting anatomical material studied in the carrel?' have been almost identical for the three years (1974-76) when this question was last asked. A mean of 7 per cent of students required 'considerable' demonstrator assistance, 27 per cent 'hardly ever' and 6 per cent 'never' required help, while the remainder (60 per cent) used the demonstrator only 'occasionally' (Table 21, item 4). These responses suggest that annotated photomicrographs are quite effective for the purpose of interpreting microscope slides.

The use of enlarged black and white, labelled photomicrographs in the carrels and study guide, and as demonstrations on the wall in the learning centre, reinforces the impressions of structure seen in microscope slides where sections have specific colour-staining cues. The application of two complementary strategies (colour, and black and white) may be very relevant to the learning of concepts in anatomy. Katzman and Nyenhuis (1972) have shown that the addition of colour to a visual image does not improve learning relevant to the *basic information* (as for example in tissue patterns in different organs), but it does provide cues for recognition and improves *learning of detail* (as in differentiation of tissues by specific dyes in microscope slides). An effective learning sequence is therefore provided in each module, from first using black and white photomicrographs to reinforce basic concepts when they are introduced (by colour-stained microscope slides) in the carrel, to finally presenting colour-slide transparencies in the tape-slide which summarizes the anatomical content in the module.

Tape-slides

The tape-slides carry colour transparencies, automatically projected to synchronize with the 'one to one' talk on the audiotape. Their main value was to offer students a review on completion of the module, and convenient material for revision. A 'general interest' tape-slide was also provided.

The twin channel, input in tandem of audiotape and visual media may be better as a teaching strategy than either used alone, because of individual learner differences resulting from differential attention, gain and retention of knowledge.

There were only a few tape-slides in the first year (1969) but during the next few years, two for each module were produced as time and availability of slides permitted. Many of the slide transparencies previously used in lectures were useful for this purpose. Tape-slides have been revised regularly, usually when more or better slides have been especially prepared.

CONCLUSIONS

Plant anatomy is particularly suited to audio-visual presentation. The student has to observe accurately what is under the microscope, to recall what he has observed, and to use his visual memory to interpret anatomical structures. Self-instruction using audio-visual media as in the audio-tutorial (A-T) approach, has many advantages over 'traditional' methods.

To keep lectures and laboratory work in step is difficult; in the carrel it is automatic and assured. The audiotape is neither a lecture nor a series of instructions: it simulates the presence of a personal tutor. The time-gap is reduced to a minimum between a problem arising in the student's mind and a solution to the problem; and by judicious Socratic questioning (either on the audiotape or in the groups), the student often finds he has solved the problem himself. Students can work at their own pace, not in the lockstep of laboratory hours; and there is flexibility about study time (the centre is open all day) which is impossible in traditional lecture and laboratory courses. Different rates of learning are accommodated by self-pacing, and active participation is essential at all stages of self-instruction. The integration of aural and visual learning increases comprehension, while self-assessment by quizzes at appropriate intervals in the study guide provides adequate feedback. The unevenness inevitable in a team of demonstrators to large classes is removed; all students receive their guidance from the same person and can without embarrassment have the guidance repeated. The commonest stumbling blocks are removed by the audiotape, for it anticipates routine questions, leaving the demonstrator to deal with more complicated or difficult ones.

The first aim of the course is to learn the necessary facts in their biological perspective. That is the prime function of the modules. Experience in the transfer of knowledge is provided by independent investigations incorporated in each module, and by one major project. Another merit of SIMIG is the continuity of thought between successive modules. This helps the student to avoid keeping the content of the modules in, so to speak, separate and unrelated packets. He is encouraged, both by tests during discussions and by final examination, to combine knowledge from the successive modules into a coherent overall view of the subject.

NOTES 1-5

1 *Excerpt from audiotape* (Module 5 Introduction to anatomy of woody plants) (italics indicate student activity)

In the last programme, we investigated the structure and function of herbaceous stems, and now we're going to look at the anatomy of woody stems. In a beaker in your carrel are two pieces of stem. One is soft, green and herbaceous. The other is hard, brown and woody. *Pick up each segment and feel the difference in flexibility.*

It's probably reasonable to expect that differences of this nature on a macroscopic scale will be reflected in differences on a microscopic scale. You can decide very simply whether or not this expectation is reasonable. *Cut thin transverse sections of each piece of stem and mount in aniline sulphate*. This specific stain for lignin stains only lignified cell-walls yellow. *Look at the two sections under the microscope and compare the relative amounts of lignified tissue in each stem.*

Turn on the tape again when you've made your observations.

There's not much doubt about it, is there? The bulk of the woody stem is yellow, so it's made up of cells with lignified walls. The herbaceous stem, by comparison, has very little lignified tissue − restricted to a peripheral ring of xylem in vascular bundles with some mechanical tissue. This is the typical pattern (as we discovered last week) of supporting tissues in the form of a hollow tube − an ideal arrangement for resisting bending stresses in herbaceous plants.

In a woody stem, the central arrangement of lignified tissues is similar to roots, which have to resist a pulling strain. How can we account for this? A large woody plant eg a tree, has to cope with greater bending and compression forces than herbaceous plants. The weight of the canopy compresses the trunk and major roots while the expanse of the canopy swaying in the wind generates enormous bending stresses especially during violent storms: yet rarely does the trunk shear − the tree bends but does not break − occasionally it is uprooted!

In a woody stem, the lignified tissue is xylem. You should confirm this now by *cutting a longitudinal section* of a small piece of your stem.

But this core of xylem has a different origin from the primary xylem of vascular bundles in herbaceous stems, which as you recall from the last module, is derived entirely from cells produced by the apical meristem. This is the meristem that accounts mainly for primary growth in length, but not for the massive increase in girth which is a feature of woody shrubs and trees. Xylem that makes up the bulk of a tree trunk is formed from another meristem, the vascular cambium. It consists of one layer of cells which form a continuous cylindrical sheet throughout the plant axis: it persists for the life of the plant.

The audiotape then gives details of the initiation of vascular cambium and subsequent secondary growth in a woody stem. The listener is directed to look, at various times, at five more illustrations (in the study guide and carrel photographs). With this theoretical background, the student is ready to embark on his own investigations.

In your carrel is a shoot of *Hydrangea*, a perennial woody shrub. *Cut sections from the apex to the base at four or five levels,* to see the stages of secondary growth. *Use fig 5.1 as a guide, also carrel photos 2, 3, 4. On the page provided (in the study guide) draw a series of map diagrams* to show these developmental stages. Then return to the audiotape.

2 The following *guidelines* were used in the preparation of the introduction to the audiotape script for Module 5 given in Note 1 above. Module 5 was selected in preference to Module 1 to show integration of material (e, below) and the more complex structure of later modules and audiotapes. (Module 1 is used in subsequent notes.)

   a Arouse the learner's interest/curiosity in the introduction.
   b Present basic concepts first with a general outline of the subject content.

c Involve the learner, as soon as possible, in some activity, and continue to integrate theory with practical work and observations throughout the programme.

d Interrupt the periods of talking (maximum of five minutes) even if only to look at a diagram, data, etc.

e Integrate material from previous programmes to give continuity eg herbaceous stems (Module 4), roots (Module 3) and tissues (Module 2)

See also Appendix C for a more comprehensive account of the preparation of audiotapes.

3 The course on anatomy of flowering plants is presented by eight *modules* in the following sequence: structure and function in 1) leaves, 2) tissues, 3) roots, 4) herbaceous stems; followed by 5) anatomy of wood (woody stems and roots); 6) anomalous structure in stems and roots; 7) the *project* on climbing stems; ecological anatomy of 8) aquatic plants, 9) plants subject to water deficiencies.

4 *Excerpt from study guide* (Module 1 Structure and function in leaves) Showing programme index, summaries of figures and photomicrographs, materials supplied in carrel and for demonstrations, objectives and learning activities.

PROGRAMME INDEX
Objectives and Learning Activites   11
Programme Summary
Part I   Leaf Morphology   13
Part II   Leaf Structure — Epidermis   14
            Factors Regulating Stomatal Movement   17
            Mesophyll Tissue of C_3 leaves   19
Part III Structure and Function in Relation to Photosynthesis   24
            The Calvin Cycle   24
            The Hatch-Slack Pathway   26
            Leaf Anatomy and C_4 Photosynthesis   28
            Relation of Structure to Function in C_4 species   31
Part IV Transpiration in Relation to Leaf Structure   33
References and List of Carrel Photographs   36
Answers to Self Quizzes   37

LIST OF FIGURES (in study guide — 15)

LIST OF PHOTOMICROGRAPHS (in study guide — 8)

MATERIALS SUPPLIED IN CARREL
Microscope slides (numbered 1-6)   Fresh specimens (7 species)

DEMONSTRATIONS
Specimens showing variation in leaf morphology, leaf modification, including insectivorous plants, leaf reductions, leaf variegation.

MICROSCOPE SLIDES	TAPE/SLIDE PROGRAMMES
Variations in leaf structures.	1 Leaf variegations; colour in leaves.
Leaf skeletons in glass.	2 Leaf anatomy.

General Instructional Objective To comprehend the structure of (mesophytic) leaves in relation to the functions of photosynthesis, gas exchange and transpiration.
Specific Objectives (12 listed)

LEARNING ACTIVITIES

i   Participate in and receive information from the audiotape in the carrel.
ii   Examine, by the methods indicated, six specimens (listed).
iii Examine demonstration slides showing variations in leaf structure.
iv   Examine demonstration plants showing variations in leaf morphology.
v   View tape/slide programmes.
vi   Read appropriate sections in the recommended text books and in the study guide; look at the selection of articles in the 'Literature' section in the Learning Centre.
vii Develop skill in cutting, by various methods, and mounting leaf sections, and become proficient in the use of the Leitz microscope, as set out in the study guide (Appendix III p.xiv)

5 *Excerpts from the study guide* (Module 1)
To illustrate format (figures omitted): integration of theory and practical work: independent investigations of demonstration and carrel material; self-quizzes.

LEAF ANATOMY IN RELATION TO C_4 PHOTOSYNTHESIS

COMPARATIVE BIOCHEMISTRY
First, a reminder about the 'Calvin Cycle' or Photosynthetic Carbon Reduction Cycle. Location: chloroplasts. The three biochemical phases in this process of carbon assimilation are carboxylation, reduction, and regeneration of CO_2 acceptor (see Fig. 1.9 for an outline of the Calvin Cycle).
  C_3Photosynthesis Plants which have only the Calvin Cycle are called C_3 plants, because the first product of carbon fixation is 3-PGA, a 3-carbon compound. Photosynthesis in these plants is referred to as C_3 photosynthesis. C_3 plants include all the species examined previously (*Ligustrum, Acalypha, Tradescantia, Eucalyptus* and *Bromus*).
  C_4Photosynthesis In many plant species (so-called C_4plants) CO_2 is not fixed into 3-PGA first, but into 4-carbon compounds called C_4-dicarboxylic acids (malate and aspartate). The enzyme involved is phospho-enol-pyruvate (PEP) carboxylase, and we can sum the reaction as: $3C + 1C = 4c$. Photosynthesis in these plants is referred to as C_4 photosynthesis. C_4 plants for examination are *Zea Mays* (Maize), *Atriplex spongiosa* (Saltbush) and *Amarantus edulis* (an ancient grain amaranth crop plant of the Americas).

C_4 photosynthesis is only known in Angiosperms (flowering plants). Most species are C_3.

C_4 species are predominantly located in tropical environments. The flora of arid environments often has a large C_4 component.

C_4 LEAF ANATOMY

The biochemical events of C_4 photosynthesis (Fig. 1.11) are cellularly compartmented. Half of the C_4 Acid Cycle occurs in one cell type (the mesophyll cells), and the other half *plus* the Calvin Cycle occur in another cell type (the 'Kranz' cells). Note that the Calvin Cycle is restricted to the Kranz cells. PEP carboxylation is restricted to mesophyll cells.

Where are the two cell compartments in C_4 plant leaves? The Kranz cells usually comprise the bundle sheath surrounding the vascular bundles, and they contain abundant chloroplasts. Atmospheric CO_2 is fixed by PEP carboxylase in the mesophyll cells, which often radiate out from the bundle sheath cells like the spokes of a wheel. This kind of leaf anatomy, referred to as 'Kranz anatomy', was the first, and is the most common kind of leaf anatomy associated with C_4 plants. ('Kranz' is German for 'wreath', referring originally just to the bundle sheath.) 'C_4 leaf anatomy' is a more general term.

Zea mays (Maize). T.S. leaf, fresh microtomed section and SLIDE 5.
Make a wet mount of *Zea mays* microtomed T.S. leaf and compare with Slide 5. Note the single bundle sheath of large parenchyma cells around the vascular bundle. The walls of this bundle sheath are fairly thick (see Fig. 1.11). Mesophyll cells surround the bundle sheath in an orderly wreath-like arrangement in which each cell is oriented with its longer diameter at right angles to the circumference of the bundle sheath (radiating mesophyll). The chloroplasts of the bundle sheath of maize and other C_4 grasses are different (usually larger and more abundant) from those of the surrounding mesophyll. In contrast, C_3 grasses such as *Bromus* have only one type of chloroplast.

Atriplex spongiosa (Saltbush). SLIDE 6.
Examine and compare with Slide 5 (above).

How to recognize C_4 plants anatomically
It is possible to identify C_4 plants from leaf-anatomical observations alone:

a   Look for 'Kranz anatomy' radiating mesophyll around a bundle sheath of chloroplast-packed cells. Look at your carrel photo p.14.

b   More reliably, for grasses at least, count the mesophyll cells between the bundle sheaths of two adjacent vascular bundles in a leaf transection. Look across a whole transection and score the maximum count (the 'maximum lateral cell count'). For grasses, this is:

$\leq$4 for C_4 species
>4 for C_3 species   } see Fig. 1.12.

3 'Unknowns' on demonstration bench:

Slide No.	Your Prediction as C_3 or C_4		Correct?	
	1 Using Kranz anatomy criteria	2 Using max. lateral cell count	1	2

Self-quiz (4)
1 Of what advantage to a C_3 dorsiventral leaf is the large volume of intercellular air space?
2 Kranz cells of C_4 species do not have much contact with intercellular air space. The Calvin Cycle in the bundle sheath of Kranz cells is dependent on free CO_2. How is this supplied?
3 List the factors or features which may account for the higher photosynthetic rate in C_4 plants under optimum conditions.
4 Photosynthesis in C_4 leaves saturates, if at all, only at full sunlight, while photosynthesis in C_3 leaves saturates at 20-35% full sunlight. Explain.

3 Tools for Learning: 2 Small Group Discussions

The aim of interactive group (IG) discussions, held for two hours each week, is to probe the students' comprehension of the module studied the previous week, and to develop those higher order cognitive skills used in solving anatomical problems. All students attend, as the groups are an integral part of the teaching/learning method, with discussion based on projected slides and printed questions, some of which are used as assessment tests.

The first part of this chapter describes the distinctive features of SIMIG groups: the introductory session; the use of media in providing structure both for discussion and for presentation of material designed to develop cognitive skills; the pattern of the question paper which incorporates tests for continuing assessment; and the role of the tutor. The second part of the chapter presents the following: an outline of the evolution of techniques used in SIMIG groups; the rationale of the group teaching/learning methods for this course; and a schematic representation of the distinctive features of the two complementary techniques of SIMIG. The notes at the end of the chapter include a group question paper (Module 1), and excerpts from transcripts of discussions of one group in their first session (on Module 1) and their final session (on Module 8).

INTRODUCING STUDENTS TO GROUP WORK

There is no learning task for the first group session (while the first module is being studied), so group members, most of whom are strangers to one another, are given several light-hearted exercises which dissolve their initial shyness. The first exercise of 'getting to know each other' is based on the 'one-to-one' interviewing technique developed by Potts (1981 p.97). In this relaxed atmosphere, individuals reveal information about themselves that they are willing to share with the group; they also have an opportunity for uninterrupted self-expression, and they learn how to listen without interrupting.

For the second exercise, group members split into sub-groups of two or three, to solve some simple non-botanical problems – one spatial mechanical and two cognitive types allowing divergent thinking. Then they compare solutions; this encourages interaction and sets the scene for subsequent group discussions.

For the final exercise the whole group sits in a semi-circle; the tutor projects some slide transparencies to illustrate the effects of a current environmental dispute (eg sand mining of beaches for minerals). Group members are asked to discuss any aspect of this that interests them. Contributions may be hesitant at first, but if the tutor patiently waits during silences the students eventually get going, with the talk becoming quite lively.

FORMAT OF DISCUSSION GROUPS
Organization
In the previous enrolment week students have been interviewed in order to book times for group meetings. A few request the same group; otherwise, individuals assigned to each group (maximum 10, minimum 7) are matched − as far as possible − for age and ability, and where practicable with equal numbers of men and women.

From 1972, groups have met in a room furnished for the specific requirements of SIMIG groups. Seating is arranged in a U shape, so that all group members have face to face contact and an unobstructed view of the two large images (2 × 1.5m) of colour slide transparencies projected on to the wall, which serves as a screen. Two auto-focus slide projectors are mounted on the opposite wall, behind the group. Projections with slide advance/reverse and room lighting are remotely controlled by the tutor from a panel on a movable desk, placed at one end of the group's tables. This arrangement ensures that the attention of the group is on the slide transparencies (automatically focused) and not distracted by the tutor 'fiddling with the hardware'.

Structure and Process
The skeleton framework for discussion is supplied by a printed question paper in association with projected slide transparencies of plant sections, some of which have been examined (as microscope slides) in the learning centre, others are previously unseen. The purpose of the questions − encompassing the objectives of the module studied the previous week − is to elicit ideas or concepts arising from the material investigated in the module. The projected transparencies supply the information or clues necessary for answering those questions: the quality of the answers depends, of course, not only on how well students have assimilated the content of the module, but on how perceptively they have comprehended the content.

Group members read the question, study the projected slide(s), then write their answers individually in the space provided (two or three lines) on their question papers. One member reads his answer to the group, and the question is open for general discussion; meanwhile the slides (usually two per question) remain projected. To ensure that a few students do not dominate the group, and that 'air time' is provided for each member, the tutor suggests that the first provisional answer to each question be given in rotation around the group. Without exception, groups have accepted this proposal, and although there is the option of 'passing' − perhaps to avoid embarrassment when unsure about a response − this is rarely taken, even by shy or insecure students. At each group meeting, members usually average two 'first' answers in addition to any other contributions made to the open discussions which follow. This exchange of opinions not only exposes and resolves difficulties, but also improves the skill of verbal communication − a desirable spin-off. As soon as there is a consensus in the group about the acceptable answers to a question, the discussion is closed. Before passing on to the next item, every member provisionally marks his own answer with a symbol (correct, incorrect or doubtful). From student opinion question-naires, this immediate feedback provides an effective way of learning.

With plant sections which have been examined previously, in the carrel, students can test out understanding of previewed material and concepts. With sections previously unseen, they can apply or transfer knowledge or concepts from 'the known' to the hitherto 'unknown'. In problem questions, the student learns to make decisions as to what is pertinent to the problem: viz. what information to use or discard from the total information presented by the slides and how to evaluate the significance of anatomical structures, eg by first using diagnostic and then supportive features.

It might be assumed that the structured format of printed question papers and discussion based on responses would result in stereotyped group discussions. But tutors have found that every group is quite different, imposing its own discipline, controlling not only the amount of discussion on each item, but generating, from the variety of responses and interchange of information and opinions, quite different aspects for discussion. Confirma-tion can be readily obtained by listening to the taped discussions, recorded — with consent of the groups — from 1976 to 1978.

Continuing Assessment

Questions for discussion only are interspersed with those requiring written answers: the latter are scored and used for continuing assessment. At the end of the session, papers are handed to the tutor for review of students' provisional marking and for the final score: every answer cannot be discussed and assessed in the group. Credit is given (by the tutors) for reasonable or plausible answers, not only for one predetermined 'right' answer. All test items, irrespective of cognitive demand, carry one or no marks.

The tests motivated individuals to complete module study before the group meeting (one week later), so that *every group member had sufficient prior knowledge to take some part in the discussion*. Individuals could also monitor their own progress as their group and class averages for weekly tests were announced at the beginning of each meeting, when each student got his test paper back.

In questionnaires about the course students have responded favourably to the use of assessment in groups. Any tendency to be anxious is reduced by 'discussion only' questions spaced at intervals. For part of the time at least, it becomes like a game, for students know that no subjective assessment is made of their contributions to group discussions: assessment is by scored answers only.

The performance of students in continuing assessment is discussed in Chapers 6 and 7.

The Question Paper

Based on the responses to these tests, I was able to monitor the efficacy of the questions I had devised. Questions which were not sufficiently discriminative were revised, others were replaced, usually as better slides became available.

The level of response to the information in a particular slide depended, of course, upon how the question was phrased. Indeed, it was the phrasing of the questions rather than the preparation of slides which took so much time, because I wanted the opportunities for answers to range from simple recall or recognition to analysis and evaluation. Cognitive demand of questions was indicated on the paper. In classifying the items to be used for tests in continuing assessment, Bloom's (1956) taxonomy of educational objectives was adopted in a modified form; separating the higher categories of intellectual skills is often difficult, especially in short answer questions. A convenient rearrangement of the six categories of Bloom's hierarchy (discussed further in Chapter 4) is: *recognition or recall of knowledge* — Category 1; *comprehension* — Category 2; *application* — Category 3; *problems* — including one or more of categories 4, 5 and 6, ie *analysis, synthesis* and *evaluation*, in addition to knowledge and skills 2, 3.

It is essential that the test paper itself should draw out the different responses necessary for these categories of skills. Therefore there has to be a *pattern to the test paper* (this chapter, Note 6). In order to loosen up discussion, each group session starts with at least one open-ended (unscored) question. Recall items of low cognitive demand usually follow: these require observation, recognition, or recall of basic concepts, which will be used throughout the group session. Misconceptions are then 'aired' and corrected early on. Subsequent items build up to more complex conceptual exercises, including exposure to unfamiliar material. Expository discussion questions (some associated with slides) are inserted between the more difficult items, eg those requiring analysis, as in simple problems.

The questions (some of which are based on repeated exposure to the same concepts) follow an ascending scale of sophistication, beginning with identification of material seen in previous modules, followed by identification of the concepts inherent in the material, later generalized by application to new material, presented as test items spaced throughout the paper. This technique of sequencing which necessitates returning to the same concepts with a variety of examples, and sometimes varying the level of cognitive demand, is well illustrated by reference to the group test paper (this chapter, Note 6) on the first module. With three pairs of transfer (application) questions, *item analysis* has shown the improvement in the percentages of correct responses, recorded at various time intervals throughout the test paper.

Role of the Tutor
The tutor's role is to keep a low profile. As a member, but not as leader of the group, the tutor promotes discussion between other members, stimulating but never dominating discussion.

Traditional lectures and tutorials predispose students to be deferential to authority. Accordingly, they expect the group tutor to assume this authoritarian role even though they were encouraged to talk with one another in the introductory groups in the first week. Until they get used to the idea, they may have to be reminded to address their remarks to their peers rather than to the tutor.

To accelerate effective group interaction during the first meeting, it is not the tutors' role to 'leap in to repair any silence' (Abercrombie 1968) but they may need to provide encouragement by supplying clues or hints. After a few weeks, most groups readily accept the reticence of tutors during discussion.

Eschewing direct intervention, the tutor can keep discussion flowing and aid the learning process by using silence and non-verbal cues, by occasionally posing a question, or by gently channelling discussion towards significant cues in the slide transparencies.

With projected slides conveying a wealth of information, the tutor is confronted by what Abercrombie (1969) describes as the dilemma of teaching: 'how to tell students what to look for without telling them what to see.' Careful phrasing of the printed question is often the answer to this dilemma. Referring back to previous remarks made by one or more group members is another way of reviving and redirecting discussion towards a possible solution.

The role of summarizing may be difficult for some groups. Particularly when requested, the tutor may find it useful to summarize, clarify or amplify discussion of a particular item (this chapter, Note 8). The extent to which the tutor needs to resort to these techniques of reinforcement depends, of course, on the particular group and the skills of its individual members.

Comparatively few transcriptions have been made of group discussions — recorded for all groups from 1976 to 1978. By listening to the tapes, it is evident that the individual style of the tutor (degree of non-intervention, skill in stimulating discussion) has a marked effect on the 'climate' of the group. From maps of interaction patterns (Bales 1951) it was established that the input of tutors decreased significantly with time.

Two excerpts from transcripts of discussion by one group (this chapter, Notes 7 and 8) illustrate a noticeable change in the attitude of group members from one of insecurity in the first 'working' group to that of confidence in the final group meeting.

EVOLUTION OF TECHNIQUES 1972-78
There is little doubt that improvements made from 1972 to 1978 in the use of media in groups, together with an increase in time spent in discussion, have provided more effective learning experiences for students. Evidence presented in Chapter 5 strongly supports the suggestion that these changes were influential in improving performance in final examinations.

Increase in Time spent in Groups
When group discussions of the SIMIG type began in 1972, they lasted for one hour, but it was clear that this was short of the optimum length. In 1976, with a decrease in the number of enrolments, it was possible to schedule meetings for one and a half hours. Sessions were extended to two hours in 1978, when it was evident that students would welcome more time for discussion; though the time allowed for completing the assessment tests was still strictly controlled.

Changes in Media used
The question papers (with spaces for short answers to items scored for continuing assessment), and the projected slide transparencies which supply the information or cues for responses, are the only media used in group discussions.

Increase in Difficulty of Weekly Tests   The mix of the four categories of test questions was progressively changed from year to year (Fig. 1). The mix in the final examination questions was also progressively changed (Fig. 3). Accordingly, both in test questions and final examinations, there was a deliberate trend of increased sophistication in the questions set, but with a consistently higher intellectual demand for final examinations.

The pattern of the test paper (as described on p. 26) was gradually refined in conjunction with the change in the mix of four categories of test items used for group discussion.

Classification (based on Bloom's hierarchy) of group test items for continuing assessment, as shown in Figure 1, was retrospectively scored by two assessors (whose judgement — tested statistically — was almost identical). The proportions of different categories of questions between years are therefore comparable.

In 1972, basic questioning was predominant in test items. With slide transparencies available for the first time in groups, it seemed desirable to use them for testing recall of knowledge and recognition of tissues in order to check students' learning of basic information from module study. Results confirmed that this type of learning had been effective, but, as one of the

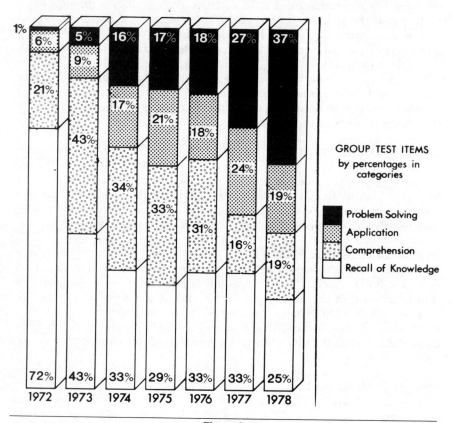

Figure 1

Percentages of all weekly test items in four cognitive categories (based on Bloom's 1956 classification, see text) used in group sessions, 1972-78.

aims was to encourage critical thinking, in the following years, 1973, the proportion of recall items was reduced (from 72 per cent to 43 per cent). Equal emphasis was placed on recall of *knowledge* and on *comprehension* (understanding), while the overall proportion of items testing *application* (transfer of information) to previously unseen material, and of short-chain *problems* was doubled. In the three succeeding years, 1974, 1975 and 1976, the proportions of test items in the more demanding categories of application were approximately doubled and problems trebled. By 1978, the proportion of short-chain problems had increased to 37 per cent. Details of the changes are summarized in Figure 1.

A comprehensive retrospective analysis of test items (prior to the 1975 intake of students) allowed the setting up of standardized (criterion referenced) tests which have been used subsequently. Weekly scrutiny of test papers (by item analysis) routinely carried out for the period 1976-78, revealed questions which were too difficult or too easy, or which did not discriminate sufficiently well between possible answers. The questions were revised each year with the specific intention of increasing the cognitive demand of test items. With a factual subject it is difficult to phrase questions to elicit a response requiring analysis or evaluation. Nonetheless, the proportions of questions testing higher cognitive skills were increased gradually, often by introducing new slides of better quality especially prepared for framing specific questions.

Increase in Number of Slides   Concurrently with the analysis of test items (Fig. 1) data relating to another variable, viz. the number of slide transparencies used in each group session, across years, was also extracted from past records and these are presented in Table 1. Not surprisingly, the number of slide transparencies used in group sessions had been increased considerably from 1972 (when they were first used) to 1978. While the average number of slides used per group had increased from 13.8 in 1972 to 43.3 in 1978, the total number per course per year had more than quadrupled (Table 1).

The bank of slides, prepared to incorporate the wealth of biological material that illustrates the diversity in plant anatomy, was put to use when it became apparent that students were learning, by exposure to such a variety of examples, the very skills needed to solve anatomical problems. Transfer of

Year	Total Slides per Group Session*							Average per Group	Total per Course
	I	II	III	IV	V	VI	VII		
1972	4	20	11	14	20	–	–	13.8	69
1973	7	24	11	16	13	–	16	14.5	87
1974	16	24	10	28	26	16	20	20.0	140
1975	33	24	15	24	26	20	28	24.3	170
1976	36	24	18	37	30	42	36	31.9	223
1977	38	28	20	44	45	64	44	40.4	283
1978	37	33	25	46	52	64	46	43.3	303

*Of the total 9 groups, the first is introductory, and in one other students present the results of a project, comparable to one module.

Table 1
Total number of slide projections used in seven group sessions, average number of slides per group and total number per course from 1972-78. In group session IV, 1975, four slides were removed from discussion and reinstated in 1976 for the experiment described in Chapter 5, p.**00**.

information, and all higher order skills practised in groups, has required a collection of slide transparencies of plant sections *previously unseen* by students. These were used to frame new questions and to challenge ideas about existing questions. Slides were sometimes used in another context, eg in group discussion at the end of a session, to reinforce particularly difficult concepts (this chapter, Note 6).

CONCLUSIONS

Rockford (1975) whimsically reflects on the task of catering for a disparate group of students: 'The realities of student life generally defeat my expectations, Mr. A. is shy, Miss B. uncooperative, Miss C. has not done the reading, and Mr. D. is somewhere else.' The format of SIMIG groups overcomes these difficulties. Attendance is regular and obligatory. No member can afford to be uncooperative because scores in the assessment tests count for half the credit toward overall course assessment.

The groups fulfil several purposes: they reinforce the discipline of observation learnt in independent study in the carrels; they help to bridge the gap between inert knowledge and genuine comprehension; they provoke students to apply their knowledge to the interpretation of hitherto unseen material; they provide practice in those higher order skills used in solving anatomical problems; and they provide an essential feedback to students for monitoring their own progress.

The printed questions and the projected slides provide a secure framework for the discussions. To begin with, each student has to tackle each question individually and to write down the answer. Once this is done it is easy to start a discussion without any need for the tutor to put the kind of probing questions that are apt to cause the insecure student to clam up. It is enough for students to be encouraged to defend what they have written. This breaks the ice and often leads to lively and illuminating talk, and to the realization that to some questions there is not one 'right' answer; indeed some students enliven the discussion by coming out with perfectly valid responses which had not previously occurred to the tutor.

There is no doubt that students understood more fully the basic concepts and principles of anatomy when, in 1972 for the first time, test items and group discussions were associated with projected slide transparencies of colour-photomicrographs of plant sections. With any microscope study, misconceptions can and do occur; every section cannot be illustrated by annotated photomicrographs. But in the groups, projected slides have the advantage that the large image can be seen by everyone at the same time. Not only seen, but commented upon by members of the group, for during discussions the six-foot pointer, or alternatively a flashlight pointer, can be passed from one student to another.

Students have the same opportunities to learn from the modules, but they bring to the discussion groups very different impressions of what they have learnt. This they soon realize; they make the refreshing discovery that the same experience affects different people in different ways. The views of other student often give them a fresh insight into the way they themselves can approach a problem. Sharing of answers, ideas and strategies promotes a more critical way of thinking (Abercrombie 1960; Barnett 1958; Beard 1972). There is evidence (see p. 76) to suggest that group solving of some problems may be superior to problem solving by most individuals; in SIMIG groups, members can explore and benefit from both experiences. Empirical testing has shown that group tasks structured by test items and requiring prior knowledge (eg from modules) are a more useful way to learn than are tasks or questions generated for discussion by group members.

Since minimum credit is given to recall of mere factual information, students are encouraged to use the information acquired in module study by applying it in a different context, or to previously unseen material (eg slides), and to solve simple anatomical problems requiring only a few operational steps. Critical thinking is encouraged by providing this practice in the skills of comprehension and application, and with the challenge presented by this approach, motivation may be stimulated and strategies for transfer learned by some, but not by all students. The ability of individual students to transfer skills and apply strategies to the solution of complex problems is not tested until the end of the course by final examination.

Student performance, even with programmed instruction, may be significantly affected by the attitudes of teachers (La Gaipa 1968; Markle 1967). SIMIG, in common with all teaching-learning methods, depends to a large extent on the people involved in teaching the course and the response of students, as learners, to personal involvement of teachers with them, as individuals. Nowhere is this more critical than in group discussion, and in SIMIG, tutors were chosen for their ability to conform to the non-authoritarian role described.

An illuminating analysis of the strategies used by tutors − in the management of syndicate groups − (Owen 1983) highlights the role of the tutor as a catalyst in contrast to less desirable behaviours. The need for staff training − not available at the University of Sydney prior to 1981 − was especially evident in group work. We instituted our own. Each week I met with one or two group tutors and together we reviewed the question paper and slides to be used, so that they were familiar with the academic content and the aims of the particular session.

There was a two-year turnover of tutors (usually young graduates with little or no teaching experience), so they were invited to preview one of my groups each week before managing their own. This gave them some idea how to facilitate peer discussion − a technique which they rapidly discovered was learnt only by experience (see tutor's report, p. 113).

By being tutor to at least half of the groups each week for ten years, I was able to make a continuing qualitative as well as objective assessment of student learning; this enabled me to improve and modify sections of the course and to refine the media, the techniques and my own style of management of the groups.

SUMMARY: THE SIMIG METHOD

The complementary strategies are to learn from the material in the modules, to deepen the comprehension of what is learnt by group discussions, to develop higher order cognitive skills (in Figure 2 represented as practice in problem-solving skills), reinforced by self-assessment by the student, with a feedback to the teacher, who can modify the curriculum in the light of the weekly tests and a final examination. Figure 2 is a schematic summary of these two teaching and learning strategies in which modules, 'programmed' to be followed without a teacher, have one 'on call', whereas in the group discussions, the role of the teacher is to promote a lively exchange between all group members. Every student is known by name by at least one tutor.

Learning strategies in SIMIG are oriented towards two types of transfer. Through self-quizzes and other self-directed activities learning is carried over from modules to groups (lateral transfer). Interaction with peers in group discussion − facilitated by media − trains students in skills required for solving short-chain problems in group tests, and for complex problems in examination (vertical transfer).

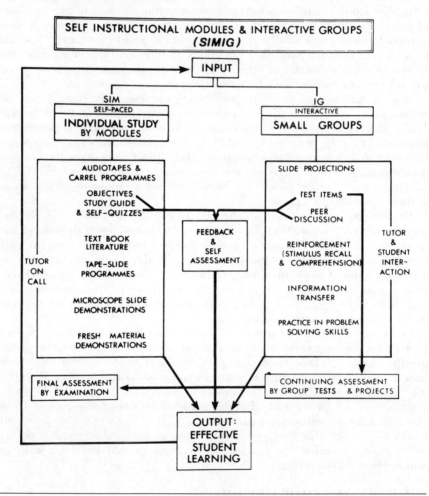

Figure 2
Diagrammatic representation of the two complementary techniques used in SIMIG, contrasting: (a) student activities; (b) roles of tutor; (c) methods of self assessment; (d) types of course assessment.

The rationale for the SIMIG method of teaching and learning is consistent with the views of educational psychology. For example Gagné and Rohwer (1969) have specified eight conditions which might be expected to improve learning. While it is not suggested that SIMIG was designed around these, in retrospect all eight are applicable to teaching strategies involving media within SIMIG. As they have been incorporated in the text of Chapters 2 and 3, it is unnecessary to repeat them here: and readers will find the full argument of this theoretical underpinning in Gagné and Rohwer's paper.

There is no doubt that the initial preparation — and monitoring of the course to effect improvements — makes heavier demands on the course organizer/programmer. Two questions therefore have to be answered: *Are the results of teaching and learning by this method sufficiently superior to warrant the extra effort involved in presentation?* and *Do the students regard SIMIG as a more effective and enjoyable way to learn?* The answers to the first question are to be found in Chapters 4 to 7, and to the second in Chapter 8.

NOTES 6-8

6 *Excerpts from the first group test paper (1977)*
Given in the second week after completion of Module 1 (Leaves). The full test paper is not printed below but the *pattern* of questions is shown, with some examples from each question type (R = recall, C = comprehension, A = application, P = simple problem). Group sessions begin with one or two unscored discussion questions followed by items requiring only recall of knowledge. Questions of higher cognitive demand follow, interspersed with less difficult questions, and some unscored discussion items. (This arrangement alleviates the build up of anxiety levels for anxious students.)

Questions 3 and 4, 16 and 17 and 23 and 24 indicate those which give practice in *application of the concept* used in answering — nine weeks later — the examination problem in Chapter 4, p. 55. See end of test paper for analysis of performance on these six items.

*	*Items for discussion only* No written answers required
1-24	*Numbered questions* Written answers marked for continuing assessment
	Write your answers in the spaces provided with blue or black ink. At the conclusion of discussion on each numbered question, mark your answer (in the margin) with a |✓, X or ? in pencil or coloured ink. No additions or corrections are to be made to your answers during or after discussion of each item. Papers are collected at the end of the group session, checked and marked by the tutor, then returned at the following group meeting.
*	In what ways is transpiration an asset/a liability to a plant?
*	Plants can absorb some water soluble sprays through their leaves. How is this achieved?
1 & 2(R)	SLIDES 1 and 2 SLIDES 3 and 4
3(A)& 4(A)	What photosynthetic pathway (C_3 or C_4) would operate in these leaves?
	Justify your answers by referring to the same two

anatomical features in each leaf section.
SLIDES 5 and 6

5(P)   You are given that (1) these two leaves (from different species) are of the *same thickness*, and (2) their photosynthetic *rates* are *identical* (ie CO_2 fixed/unit leaf area/unit time). Which of the 3 mesophyll types of tissue present assimilate/fix carbon at the fastest rate; rank them in order 1, 2, 3.

6(C)   Wilting is due to certain changes in leaf tissue caused by water stress. Which tissue is most affected?

7 & 8(R)   What is the mechanism of wilting? How does it differ from plasmolysis?
SLIDES 7 and 8
These are transverse sections of a sun and shade leaf from the same species; the upper surface is at the top of each slide.

9(C)   Is Slide 7 a shade or a sun leaf?

10(C)   On which feature(s) do you base your conclusion?

*   SLIDE 9 (10 blank)

11(R) & 12(C)   SLIDES 11 and 12

*   SLIDES 13 (14 blank)

13(P)   SLIDE 15 (16 blank)

*   SLIDES 17 and 18
SLIDES 19 and 20

14(R)   What are the structures indicated by the cavities in the leaf mesophyll?

15(P)   Given a whole leaf, how could you verify your answer?

16 & 17(A)   What photosynthetic pathway (C_3 or C_4) operates in each leaf? Justify your answers.

*   SLIDES 21 to 24

18(P)   SLIDE 25 (26 blank)

19(P)   SLIDES 27 and 28

20 & 21(R)   SLIDES 29 and 30
SLIDE 31 (32 blank)

22(P)   Leaves of the waterlily were coated with vaseline as follows:
(1) control (no vaseline); (2) on lower surface only; (3) on upper surface only. Results obtained for rates of gas exchange were: 1 = 2 = 3, 1 = 2>3, 1>2 = 3, 1>2>3 (cross out 3 and justify your answer).
SLIDES 33 and 34 (fluorescent labelled)

23 & 24(A)   Determine whether these two leaf sections have Kranz or non-Kranz anatomy.

*   SLIDES 35 to 43 (C_3 or C_4 photosynthetic pathway)
43 slides minus 5 blank = 38 total
(as shown for Module 1, 1977 in Table 1)

Analysis of responses to application items in the test paper above
The relevance of reinforcement of one concept, as a prerequisite for transfer of learning, is shown by the results of item analysis (tabled below) on six application items. Using previously unseen slides with wide

biological variation, the percentages of correct responses (for the total 1977 cohort) increased significantly during the 1½ hours of group discussion.

question numbers	3 and 4		16 and 17		23 and 24	
% correct responses	53%	72%	85%	83%	90%	93%

7 *Excerpts from transcript of a group discussion* (The first working group on Module 1) (IMB = tutor; S = student)

IMB As I have explained to you previously, we use the group recordings to analyse interaction patterns, and to see if these change across the eight weeks. Hopefully, you will all talk more and learn more, while I will talk less and less! ... *Laughter*
So let's start the first discussion question:
In what ways is transpiration an asset/liability to a plant? (see group question paper in Note 6)

S5 It's a liability because it's a danger the plant will dry up. ... *Laughter*

S3 It's an asset because it brings up water and ions to the plant and also it's some sort of cooling system as the water evaporates from the leaves.

IMB May I remind you, please, to direct your comments to the whole group, as you did last week (in the brief discussion on sand-mining) and not specifically to me!

S6 And it draws the nutrients from the soil up through the xylem. ...

IMB (After long silence) Can anyone add anything else?

S9 With excessive water loss, the stomata will close... photosynthesis will be limited by the availability of CO_2 in the internal air spaces...

S4 Loss of water is a liability if it results in temporary or permanent wilting.

The interaction so far was good. Later, there was hesitancy with some items, requiring input from me. I also continued to give suggestions about peer-management of the group, to which they responded quite well, eg taking turns in providing the first answer to each question, by reading their written responses (group members appeared to like this novel suggestion).

S8 I'll start then (Questions 14 and 15, p. 34) ... I said the structure was an oil gland, does anyone agree with that? *Three students agree*. I don't know how you do it though, that is verify it, mash it up I suppose and get the contents out of the oil glands. *Several students comment — inaudible.*

S1 You could crush it and smell the Eucalyptus oil.

S4 Hold it up to the light and see the oil glands.

IMB Suggests cutting a section; staining with an oil-specific stain.

Subsequent discussion of two application questions (Questions 16 and 17, p. 34).

What is the photosynthetic pathway (C_3 or C_4) in these two leaves? (See Note 5, pp. 20 - 21: difference between C_3 and C_4 leaves)

S9   Well, it's my turn,... are we all ready? I don't know the answers really... Slide 20 I thought was a C_3. I thought that there was more than the maximum cell count between the veins (bundles). Whereas Slide 19 on maximum cell count should be a C_4.

S3   But you only use maximum cell count for grasses, and these aren't grasses, are they?

S5   With Kranz anatomy there's radiating mesophyll... there's none in these sections, so they must both be C_3.

S2   Why is maximum cell count used only with grasses?

After further discussion and some confusion I decided to provide some input. Particularly in the first few group sessions, the tutor has to judge when it is best to keep silent and when it is essential to provide reinforcement and clarification. Clearly this input was useful: in subsequent questions this group had no further problems in distinguishing C_3 from C_4 anatomy.

8 *Excerpts from transcript of a group discussion* (The last working group in Week 9 − with the same nine students) (S = student; IMB = tutor)
Question for open discussion with two slide transparencies: 'Are there any features in these sections to indicate the habitat of the plant?'

S1   The large air canals in the lower half of the section are typical of hydrophytes (water plants).

ALL S   Give non-verbal assent.

Scored problem question: 'Is there evidence to identify these sections as floating leaves?' (Students observe slides and write their answers)

S4   Well, it's my turn. I said yes, and the reason was that there is photosynthetic tissue as one would expect in a floating leaf.

S5   Yes, it's palisade tissue, typical of the upper surface of many leaves.

S2   The pattern of tissue is very similar to the floating leaf of water lily we examined in last week's module.

S6   I'd agree that it's a floating leaf.

S7   So do I!

S3   I'm not so sure. What's on the lower surface?

S8   It must be lower epidermis.

S3   Well it doesn't look like that to me.

S4   The cells look squashed...

S9   If this were a leaf, wouldn't the xylem be above the phloem in the leaf veins?

S1   Yes, of course you're right! It's the other way round.

S6   So, it can't be a leaf − the position of xylem and phloem is typical of stems.

S5   Yes, it must be a stem! The evidence is there alright, but most of us didn't use it.

S9   Perhaps it's the outer part of the stem of a rush, growing on the water's edge.

S8   I haven't seen photosynthetic tissue like that in any
                       stem, only in leaves. ...
I.M.B.   Yes, it is the hollow stem of a rush. That's why the
                       lower surface didn't look like the lower epidermis of a
                       leaf — it's the tissue lining the central cavity of the stem.
                       The palisade tissue is a bit of a red herring! (Projects a
                       section of floating leaf of water lily)
                       Here's the leaf of *Nymphaea*, the water lily you
                       examined last week. When you compare the two, the
                       palisade tissue is very similar in both, but the position
                       of xylem in the vascular bundle is the *diagnostic* feature,
                       as you can see now with sections of stem and leaf side
                       by side.

It is apparent from the above transcript that students were controlling this
group discussion. They rapidly dismissed the comprehension question and
immediately turned their attention to the problem question. After a false
start in open discussion, and hesitancy by some members, they finally solved
the problem by themselves. With the aid of an additional slide, the tutor
provided reinforcement prior to closure of this item — to remove any
lingering doubts (eg Student 8).

4 Methods of Assessment: 1 Final Examinations

INTRODUCTION

Formal education is one of Man's most ancient activities. In the Talmud, written some 2000 years ago, there are precise instructions about student-teacher ratios in schools. So it is not surprising that novel strategies for learning are regarded with suspicion, and it is essential to justify any novel strategy by a rigorous evaluation of its worth. That is, perhaps, the useful contribution this book has to make. This chapter presents the evidence accumulated systematically, from final examinations over the period of the study (1969-78).

Performance in the final examination is the generally accepted criterion of achievement. There are two aspects of this: the nature of the questions posed, ie of the knowledge and skills required in the examinations; and the performance of the students in the various components. Much of the evidence assembled here consists of a rigorous statistical analysis of the examination results and of the factors which might be expected to influence them. But since the detailed statistics are likely to be of limited interest to the general reader I have adopted the policy of presenting the conclusions, accompanied by some simplified tables and diagrams, in the main body of the chapter, and placing the methodological analysis in the notes at the end of the chapter. The same presentation is also adopted in subsequent chapters.

Course Assessment

Course assessment was determined by combining scores from two types of assessment, viz. continuing, or formative assessment from weekly test scores, and summative assessment from final examination scores. Prior to 1972 continuing assessment counted only 15% towards course assessment; but from 1972 (when the SIMIG style groups were introduced) students were assessed by combining, with equal weighting, both types of assessment. There were two reasons in 1972 for introducing this higher rating for continuing assessment: first, in response to students' requests in the early seventies, the university had asked departments to decrease the loading on final examinations (and as far as possible to hold them at the end of the term in which the course was given); second, I wanted to make sure that students attended groups regularly, as I firmly believe that real learning takes place far better where students interact with one another and their teacher. With a

50% weighting on weekly test scores, students felt obliged to attend group sessions. In the event, most students worked hard to score well; they also learnt a lot, most of them apparently enjoyed the experience, and later affirmed that they would have attended even if the group tests had not been scored for assessment (Table 22, item 16).

The relatively low weighting of 50% given to final examination scores in this course in no way diminishes the importance that I attach to them, for the two types of assessment make different intellectual demands (as can be seen from a comparison of Figs. 1 and 3). Especially from 1974, final examinations were essentially a test of problem solving. Continuing assessment, while predominantly testing lower order skills, at the same time provided the basic training needed by the students if they were to be able to bridge the gap demanded by the type of complex problem questions used in examination.

Cohorts 1969-78

In Australia, the academic year runs from February to November. At the University of Sydney it is divided into three terms of nine weeks.

Successive cohorts of students were tested in the Faculties of Science (1969-78) and Agriculture (1969-75) at the University of Sydney, reading for a BSc (three-year) or BScAg (four-year) degree. These students completed a nine-week course in plant anatomy, representing one-third of the botany strand in second-year biology. The sample size varied from 1969 to 1975 (n~90-120), but subsequently decreased (n~70-80) when in 1976 a change in the agriculture curriculum resulted in withdrawal of students from this faculty.

As some of the variation in performance in examination is due to fortuitous variation of the cohorts, it will be useful to consider first how general ability in any one cohort was determined, and which years are comparable, according to the tests used.

Three standardized test scores were used from 1974 as the basis for comparison of cohorts:

  1 Higher School Certificate (HSC) and matriculation examination used
     for entry to university.

			Mean Scores ± SD		
Subjects	1974	1975	1976*	1977*	1978*
HSC (aggregate)	572 ± 38	570 ± 35	549 ± 46	574 ± 42	542 ± 45
Preceding Year (%)**	58.4 ± 6.9	58.3 ± 6.5	52.1 ± 10.9	58.4 ± 7.9	53.4 ± 8.2
Biology I (%) (pre-requisite)	60.8 ± 7.7	60.9 ± 7.2	57.7 ± 10.3	62.9 ± 8.4	56.9 ± 7.9

*Marks for HSC (Higher School Certificate) adjusted to previous marking systems (maximum 850 up to 1975).
**First-year students are required to take four subjects; most students take mathematics, physics, chemistry and biology, although Biology I may also be taken as a subject in second year.

Table 2
Prior academic performance of students enrolled for SIMIG courses 1974-78. Mean scores as aggregates for HSC, percentages for other scores, ± standard deviation.

2   Biology I examination, a prerequisite for the plant anatomy course.
3   Mean score for the preceding year: usually of four science subjects taken in first year.

Table 2 shows the results of these three tests.

The ability of cohorts, as judged by these tests, was indeed different, and showed that although the cohorts of 1974, 1975 and 1977 were all comparable, the cohorts of 1976 and 1978 were statistically (this chapter, Note 9) below the rank of the above cohorts in each of the three criteria.

Comparisons therefore have been made between two pairs of cohorts: (i) 1975 and 1977, and (ii) 1976 and 1978, which were similar in quality on the basis of these three standardized test scores. Other results, from multiple regression analyses, have indicated further specific differences between these pairs of samples. Results from 1969-73 were also comparable with each other.

The age range was from 18 to 30 years (predominantly 18 - 21 years), and the sex ratio analysed for the 1975 − 78 cohorts was male to female of 3 : 2.

From 1974, a reference test in plant anatomy (see Appendix A: Records and Tests) was administered immediately prior to the course as a pre-test, and at the end as a post-test. Pre-test scores (Table 3) were all low, not surprisingly as plant anatomy was not covered in the prerequisite course in Biology I.

Year	n*	Percentage Correct Answers	
		Pre-test	Post-test
1974	105	6.4	75.0
1975	101	7.0	76.4
1976	71	7.0	76.4
1977	76	6.8	78.7
1978	65	6.9	77.5

*Includes all students with both test results.

Table 3

Performance on a reference test (mcq) in plant anatomy, given prior to (pre-test) and on completion of (post-test) a nine-week course.

CRITERIA OF ASSESSMENT
Parameters of Assessment by Final Examination

One week following the end of the course, student performance was measured in a three-hour final exmination which, as it always had been, was an 'open book' test. Students have been allowed to bring text books, but I have found that because of the type of questions asked, books have been of limited value and in fact very little used. But they do serve a useful purpose in lessening the anxiety experienced by many students during examination. As previous examination papers were not published (discriminating questions in a factual subject are difficult to set in a problem format; and all questions in fact involved practical material for inspection), it was therefore possible to retain some questions for several years, allowing comparison of results between years.

Final examinations retained the same format throughout the period of study, although their content became increasingly demanding (see Fig. 3). Short answer questions, related to specimens or slides, have been used since

1965, providing a relevant basis for comparison throughout the evolution of this method (particularly for criterion testing of the problem-solving questions introduced in 1971). Examination marking was consistent over the period: questions have been marked on a point score basis independently by two assessors whose judgement, statistically assessed, was very nearly identical. Statistical evidence shows that the examinations were reliable (this chapter, Note 10). By inspection they were also relevant to the material taught.

Use of Bloom's Taxonomic Criteria in Assessment
Bloom's (1956) taxonomy of cognitive objectives has been used as the basis for analysis of the final examination (summative assessment), and also for weekly test scores (formative assessment). Examination questions and weekly test items were classified in four cognitive categories: knowledge, comprehension, application and problem-solving. The first three correspond to Bloom's cognitive taxonomy. The first, *knowledge*, was used specifically with reference to remembering, either by recall or recognition, ideas (concepts), material, facts, etc. The second, *comprehension*, refers to the capacity for understanding – eg concepts, principles, etc. – ie apperceptive knowledge. In the third category, *application*, known facts, concepts or principles were applied to situations other than the one in which the item of knowledge was first presented. In most instances, this involved confrontation with unfamiliar, ie previously unseen, biological material. The criterion chosen to distinguish a *problem* question was that it involved, in addition to comprehension and application, one or more of the skills of *analysis, synthesis* and *evaluation* (Bloom's fourth, fifth and sixth categories). Thus problem questions need several operational steps for solution. Whereas simple problems – which can be solved in a few minutes – were used in discussion questions, the complex examination problems required multiple steps and 15 to 20 minutes for solution. Inevitably, recall of knowledge was essential for answering any question, because in a factual subject such as plant anatomy, basic knowledge is a pre-requisite for the use of other cognitive skills: ie the higher levels in Bloom's taxonomy subsume the lower ones.

Difficulty of the Examination 1969-1978
During the evolution of the SIMIG method (1969 - 78), the proportions of cognitive categories used in assessment by examination were progressively changed (Fig. 3), as they were also in continuing assessment (Fig. 1).

The percentage marks contributed by the different categories of questions in examination (Fig. 3) were predetermined and used in yearly analysis of examination scores. In 1973, questions which tested only ability to recall knowledge were phased out. Thus, from 1973, performance has been assessed in the final examination by two types of questions: (1) those requiring a combination of the skills of application and comprehension, with emphasis on application, and (2) complex problems, requiring multiple steps and 15 to 20 minutes for solution.

The examinations were made progressively more difficult over the years, by increasing the number and percentage marks awarded to problem questions, from 26% in 1971 to 80% in 1978. The marks for application/comprehension questions were adjusted as necessary (Fig. 3).

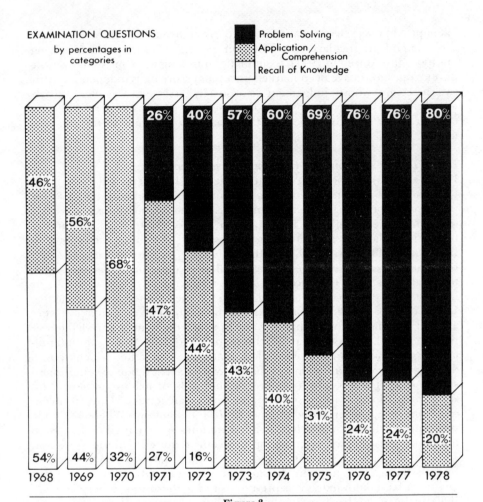

EXAMINATION QUESTIONS
by percentages in
categories

- ■ Problem Solving
- ▨ Application/ Comprehension
- □ Recall of Knowledge

Figure 3
Percentages of questions classified in three cognitive categories (based on Bloom, 1956) used in final examination, 1968-78.

Parameters of Examination	1974	1975	1977	1978
	n=105	n=115	n=76	n=65
% P questions in exam	60	69	76	80
% A/C questions in exam	40	31	24	20
No. of P questions	4	6*	6	6
No. of A/C questions	5	5	4**	4

*By reducing the marks contributed by the four problems retained from the 1974 examination, two more problems were introduced in 1975.
**Reductions in percentage marks, and in number of A/C questions in 1977, allowed further increases in the weighting of problem questions.

Table 4
Parameters of examinations from 1974 to 1978, showing for each year: the percentage marks awarded to problem-solving questions (P), and to questions combining application and comprehension (A/C); and the number of questions in each category.

Table 4 gives some indication of how this progressive change in the proportions of categories was organized from 1974 to 1978, the period for which many comparisons of performance have been made. (In all final examinations, the total possible mark was 100, so that students' scores were also percentages.)

Evidence for using the proportion of problem questions in examination, as a reliable index of difficulty, is provided by Table 5 and Note 19. Table 5 shows that from 1969-72 students had more difficulty in responding correctly to questions with a higher cognitive demand, and especially to the problem question (number 7) introduced in 1971, which required a chain of reasoning following the exercise of the capacities of recall, identification and application. It is significant that in 1972 — with the new type of group discussion — the proportions of students passing and failing this problem were reversed, together with a marked improvement in performance of the application/comprehension questions.

Categories of Examination Questions	Fail <50% Pass >50%	Percentage Students				Average Increase per Year in % pass rate*
		1969	1970	1971	1972	
		n=119	n=127	n=118	n=108	
1 Recall	Fail	6	10	11	6	–
	Pass	94	90	89	94	
2 Recall	Fail	3	7	3	1	–
	Pass	97	93	97	99	
3 Recall	Fail	4	13	1	2	–
	Pass	96	87	99	98	
4 Application/ Comprehension	Fail	36	34	40	14	4.5 ± 1.9
	Pass	64	66	60	86	
5 Application/ Comprehension	Fail	43	46	37	16	8.8 ± 2.0
	Pass	57	54	63	84	
6 Application/ Comprehension	Fail	48	43	28	22	8.9 ± 2.0
	Pass	52	57	72	78	
7 Problem	Fail	–	–	74	25	49.6 ± 6.7
	Pass	–	–	26	75	

*probability values are given in Note 11.

Table 5
Performance in seven examination questions during the four-year period 1969-72. Percentage of students passing and failing in each question shown for each year, with the average increase per year in percentage pass rate.

It is demonstrated in Note 19 that within the years from 1974 to 1978 (except for 1977) scores for examination problems were significantly less than for application/comprehension questions, ie problems were more difficult.

One examination problem, introduced in 1975, and the steps required for its solution are given in Notes 12 and 13. Less complex problems were set prior to 1974. From 1974, performance in the final examination may be regarded as a measure of the students' capacity to solve problems in plant anatomy, and was therefore a test of the efficacy of the two techniques of teaching and learning used in SIMIG.

ANALYSIS OF EXAMINATION SCORES 1968-78

Retrospective analyses, particularly of individual examination questions, were possible because scores and examination scripts of all students (more than 1000) were kept from 1968 to 1978, together with the point score marking systems for all questions.

Changes in Performance of Cohorts across Years

The prime interest for the teacher is to know whether the SIMIG method decreases the failure rate and increases the percentage of students in a cohort who reach 'mastery' (Bloom 1968) in the final examination; the criterion set for this course was a score of 80%.

Table 6 shows mean class scores from 1968 to 1978, together with percentages of students failing, those achieving mastery, and the teaching method.

Year	Teaching Method	Number of Students	Means of Class Scores	% with Mastery (80%)	% Failing (<50%)
1968	Trad.	92	60.7*	2.1** ⎫	16.4***
1969	SIM	119	70.7*	21.9** ⎭	2.5***
1970	SIM	127	67.7	19.7	8.6
1971	SIM	118	63.8*	16.2** ⎫	7.6
1972	SIMIG	108	71.5*	28.7** ⎬	7.4
1973	SIMIG	94	67.4	12.7** ⎭	7.4
1974	SIMIG	105	66.7	12.4** ⎫	9.4
1975	SIMIG	115	69.3	25.2** ⎭	8.6
1976	SIMIG	71	69.9*	22.5** ⎫	2.8
1977	SIMIG	76	74.2*	39.5** ⎬	3.9
1978	SIMIG	65	72.9	30.8 ⎭	3.0

Table 6

Summary of performance in final examinations from 1968 to 1978, showing: number in each cohort; means of class scores; percentage with mastery (80% or >); percentage failing (<50%); and teaching method (1968 traditional method; 1969-71 self-instructional modules: SIM; 1972-78 self-instruction and interactive groups: SIMIG). Significantly different (at 5 per cent level) values were obtained between successive pairs of cohorts for: means of class scores* (1968/69, 1971/72, 1976/77); for proportions with mastery** (1968/69, 1971/72/73, 1974/75, 1976/77) and for proportions failing*** (1968/69).

In Figure 4 the area of each circle represents the percentage of the cohort gaining mastery, and the shadings show the percentage content of the examination, analysed in terms of Bloom's categories, as modified for this course (data from Fig. 3 and Table 6). It is evident that although the difficulty of the examination had increased (judged by percentage of problems) there had been an overall improvement in performance at mastery level across the eleven years, but with fluctuations in performance, so that four phases of improvement are distinguishable: between the years (cohorts) of 1968 and 1969; 1971 and 1972; 1974 and 1975; and 1975 and 1977 (this chapter, Notes 14, 15 and 16).

Considering the degree of sophistication of the examination questions used during the last four years of course analysis to 1978, it was rewarding to find the increase in the percentage of students achieving overall mastery in the pairs of cohorts of comparable ability, viz. from 25 to 40 per cent in 1975 and 1977, and from 22 to 31 per cent in 1976 and 1978 (this chapter, Note 17).

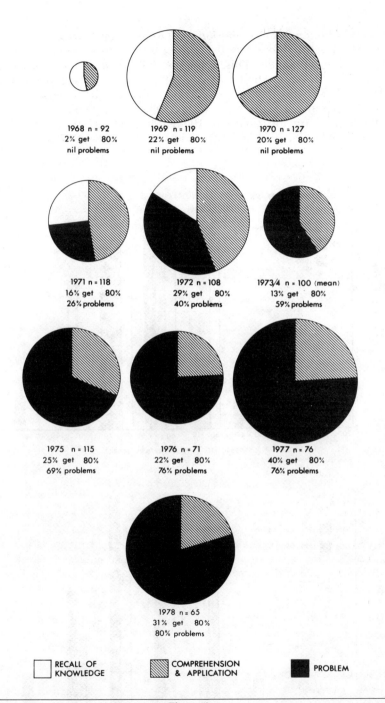

1968 n = 92
2% get 80%
nil problems

1969 n = 119
22% get 80%
nil problems

1970 n = 127
20% get 80%
nil problems

1971 n = 118
16% get 80%
26% problems

1972 n = 108
29% get 80%
40% problems

1973/4 n = 100 (mean)
13% get 80%
59% problems

1975 n = 115
25% get 80%
69% problems

1976 n = 71
22% get 80%
76% problems

1977 n = 76
40% get 80%
76% problems

1978 n = 65
31% get 80%
80% problems

☐ RECALL OF
KNOWLEDGE

▨ COMPREHENSION
& APPLICATION

■ PROBLEM

Figure 4
Diagrammatic representation of performance at mastery level in examinations from 1968
to 1978. The area of the circle represents the percentage of students with mastery (80%).
The shadings represent percentages in three categories of examination questions:
percentage problems (index of difficulty); recall of knowledge (phased out in 1973): and
application/comprehension, modified from Bloom's (1956) classification (see text).

Changes in Frequency Distributions of Examination Scores

Another feature of interest for the teacher is the distribution curve of marks in the final examination. This, generally, falls on a 'normal' (bell shaped) curve. If the SIMIG method is a more efficient way to learn, one indication of this would be a distribution curve 'skewed' to the right (ie negatively).

The histograms in Figures 5 to 8 show relative frequency distributions of examination scores for cohorts in 1968, 1969 and 1970 (Fig. 5); 1971 and 1972 (Fig. 6); 1973, 1974 and 1975 (Fig. 7), and 1976, 1977 and 1978 (Fig. 8).

5

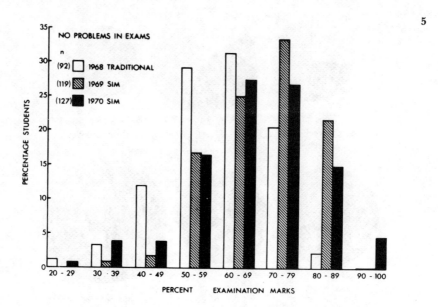

6

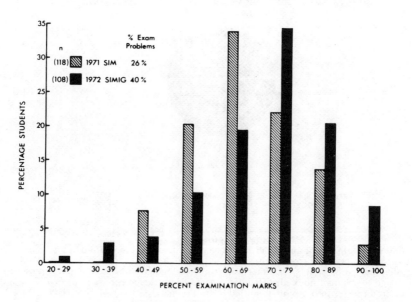

7

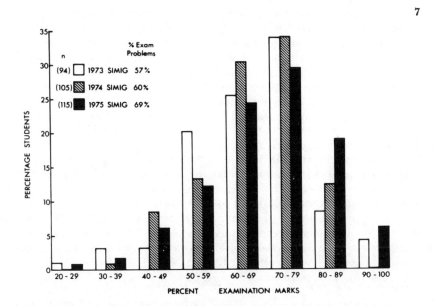

8

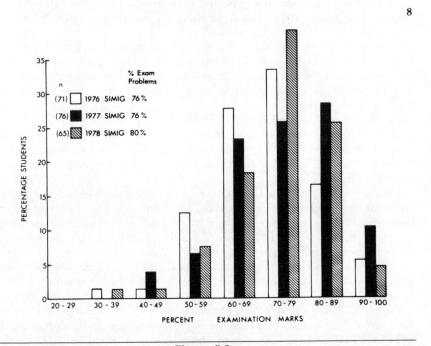

Figures 5-8
Relative frequency distributions of scores in examination over the years 1968 to 1978.
Shown for each figure: the number of students in each cohort; the teaching method –
traditional (1968), SIM or self-instruction by modules (1969-71), SIMIG or self-instruction
by modules and interactive groups (1972-78); the percentage problems in each year (index
of difficulty); black shading of histograms represents the most negatively skewed
distribution in each year/figure.

The chief conclusions may be summarized as follows.

Figure 5 shows that for the last year of traditional teaching in 1968, the distribution was roughly normal — as it was for previous years from 1965 to 1968 — and negatively skewed for 1969 when self-instructional modules were introduced. With the same teacher and an almost identical examination (see Fig. 3), the percentage of students gaining mastery (this chapter, Note 14) increased from 2 to 22 per cent and the mean class score increased by 10 per cent (Table 6). Similar skewed results in 1970, and the continued overall improvement in subsequent years, should dispel the possibility of this being due to the Hawthorne effect (Gephart and Antonoplos 1972).

Co-incident with the introduction of problem-solving questions in 1971 (26% of the total examination marks), the frequency distribution reverted to approximately normal (Fig. 6). Many students scored low marks in these problems, others did not attempt them — they were at a loss to know even how to approach them (this chapter, Note 15). In 1972 although the proportion of problem questions was increased to 40 per cent, the frequency distributions were again skewed (Fig. 6) and the percentage of students attaining mastery level was higher (29 per cent) than ever before (see Fig. 4 and Table 6). This resulted in a more pronounced degree of skew than in 1970.

It might be argued that the improved examination results in 1972 could have been because students expected problem-solving questions and were prepared to answer them; but since the final examination papers were not published (and all questions involved practical material for inspection), the 1971 examination could not in fact be used by students as a guide for 1972. It therefore seems reasonable to ascribe the higher level of examination performance to the experience gained in 1972 in the new type of SIMIG groups, where discussion questions were associated with slide projections of relevant plant sections.

Comparison of the relative frequency distributions in Figure 7 shows a definite improvement in examination performance from 1974 to 1975 (this chapter, Note 16), with a marked increase in the degree of negative skew resulting from a doubling of the percentage of students gaining overall mastery (Fig. 4, Table 6).

Frequency distributions for 1976 (Fig. 8) were again skewed, and almost identical to those for 1975 (this chapter, Note 17). But the most notable feature illustrated by Figure 8 is the extreme degree of skew in the frequency distributions of scores in 1977 and 1978, with 40 and 31 per cent respectively of the cohorts gaining mastery (Table 6). Thus in 1977/78 — the last two years of the analysis — examination performance surpassed that of all previous years, although at course entry the 1978 cohort was judged to be less competent than the cohort of 1975.

From 1975 the skewed distribution of the examination scores became more markedly negative across years. When frequency distributions for 1977 and 1978 were replotted in ranges of five centiles (rather than deciles), the resulting distributions became bimodal (Fig. 9), with two peaks of high frequency in each cohort. The significant difference (15 per cent) between the mode (most frequent score) for 1977 (85-89 per cent) and 1978 (70-74 per cent) reflects the difference in ability of these two cohorts (Table 2).

Both of the second 'peaks' in these bimodal distributions (Fig. 9) occur

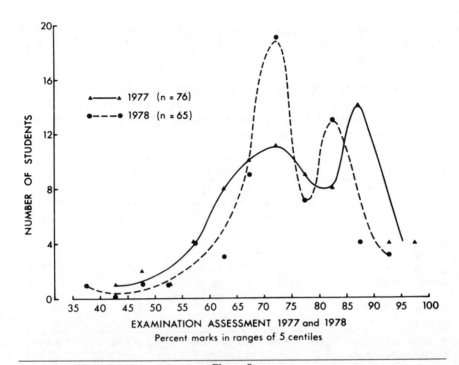

Figure 9
Negatively skewed, bimodal frequency distribution of actual scores (in ranges of 5 centiles)
gained in examination in 1977 (n=76) and 1978 (n=65). The two points of highest
frequency ('modes') are 15% apart in 1977, and 10% in 1978.

from 80 to 95 per cent; ie they represent students who, in gaining overall
mastery in examination, have also demonstrated their superior capacity for
solving anatomical problems, which, in 1977, contributed 76%, and in 1978,
80% of the total examination marks. Of course, some of the students
represented in the first peaks − with scores from 65% to 75% − would have
achieved mastery in one or more of the six problems and/or the four
application/comprehension questions set in these examinations (Table 4).

The different kinds of students represented in the first and second
distribution peaks in 1977 are shown in Figure 19.

Similar skewed, bimodal curves had been observed for frequency
distributions in *individual problems* in examination since 1975, but not for
overall examination performance in 1975 or 1976. The point score marking
system effectively discriminates between those students who solve the
problem, or who score 80% or more (first peak), and the rest (second peak
and tail) who complete only some steps or sections of its solution (see Note
13 for steps in analysis of one problem).

It is interesting to note that after my retirement in 1979, when all the same
materials (modules, group test papers, examination questions) were used,
examination results were similar to those of 1978, with a skewed, bimodal
frequency distribution.

There is no doubt that there was an overall improvement in examination
performance during the period of analysis (1974-78), even though the
examinations had become progressively more difficult by increasing the

marks contributed by problem questions from 26% in 1971 to 80% in 1978 (Fig. 3). The question arises, was this due to higher achievement levels in problem-solving questions?

PERFORMANCE IN EXAMINATION PROBLEMS 1971-78
There was an overall improvement in performance in examination problems from 1971 to 1978 with the percentage of students passing (>50%) showing a highly significant increase (this chapter, Note 18).

% Scores (deciles) in Problem Questions	Percentage of Students			
	1974*	1975*	1977*	1978
	n=105 60% Problems in Exam	n=115 69% Problems in Exam	n=76 76% Problems in Exam	n=65 80% Problems in Exam
20 - 29	3	1	–	–
30 - 39	4	3	1	1
40 - 49	13	10	3	3
50 - 59	19	16	8	14
60 - 69	**32**	24	21	25
70 - 79	27	**29**	21	**35**
80 - 89	2	12	**33**	19
90 - 100	–	5	13	3
% Means ± S E	60.0 ± 1.45	67.3 ± 1.53	75.2 ± 1.81	70.4 ± 1.70

*Cohorts of comparable ability.

Table 7

Means ± S E and relative frequency distribution as percentages of students (in deciles) of scores gained in problem questions in examination for the years 1974, 1975, 1977 and 1978. For each cohort, the number of students and the percentage of marks contributed by problems are shown, with modes indicated by heavy type.

Table 7 shows that across the years 1974, 1975 and 1977 (cohorts of comparable ability), the mean percentage scores for problems have increased significantly (this chapter, Note 19) from 60% to 75% (irrespective of a 16 per cent increase contributed by problems to examination). For the 1976 and 1978 comparable pair of cohorts (but of lesser ability), the mean percentage score for problems in 1976 was similar to that for 1975, but in 1978 performance surpassed that of all other years, with the exception of 1977 (Table 7).

Frequency distributions of scores (Fig. 10) in problems for 1974, 1975 and 1977 illustrate that although all distributions are skewed, the mode − the most frequent score − has advanced steadily from the decile group of 60 - 69% in 1974 to 80 - 89% in 1977.

Note 19 shows that while the increase in percentage scores for problems is highly significant between the years 1974/75 and 1975/77, there is a corresponding decrease (not significant) in the percentage scores attained in application/comprehension questions. This is clear evidence that, across the years analysed, improvement in overall examination scores is the result of improved performance in examination problems.

Overall Mastery/Failure in Problems
It is convenient to consider *scores in all problems* and achievement in *individual problems* at two levels: percentage of students gaining *mastery* (80%) and

percentage of students *failing* (<50%). The remainder, therefore, of the percentage passing is included to demonstrate the efficacy of the teaching method across the entire student population.

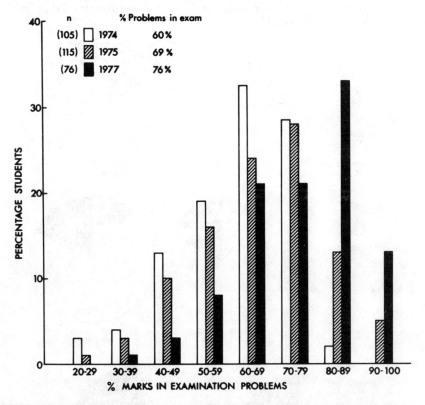

Figure 10
Relative frequency distribution of percentage scores (in deciles) for the category of problem questions in the 1974, 1975 and 1977 examinations. Percentage problems contributed to examination each year and number of students in each cohort are shown.

Using these parameters, performance in problem-solving for eight years, during the period from 1971 to 1978, is summarized in Figure 11. As problems used prior to 1974 were less complex, ie less difficult, than those set from 1974, the percentage of students with mastery in problems shown for the years 1971-73 (Fig. 11) are certainly not comparable with the mastery levels shown for the years 1974-78. By inspection, the difficulty of individual problems was also increased gradually from 1974 to 1978 by various additions and refinements.

In Figure 11 three distinct phases of *improvement* (this chapter, Note 20) are apparent: from 1971 to 1972, from 1974 to 1975, and from 1975 to 1977. Dramatic decreases in the percentage of students failing (from 75 per cent in 1971 to 4 per cent in 1977 and 1978) are accompanied by *highly significant* (this chapter, Note 21) *increases* in overall mastery of problem questions over the years: from 1 to 12 per cent (1971/73); from 2 to 17 per cent (1974/75) and from 17 to 46 per cent (1975/77). Although the (comparable) cohorts of 1976/78 were judged to be less competent than those of 1974/1975/1977 (Table 2), the results for 1976 are not significantly different from those of 1975. Performance in 1978 with 22 per cent mastery and 4 per cent failure in problems again shows an improvement on previous years, with the exception of 1977.

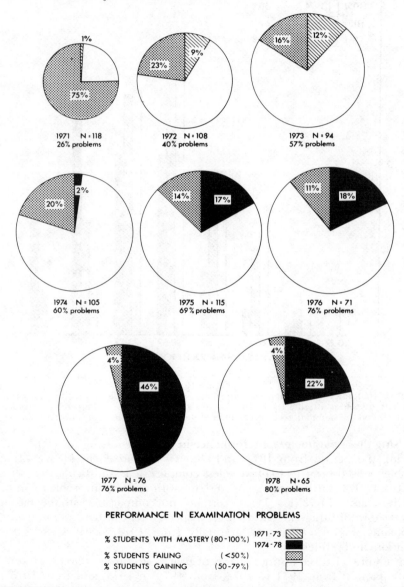

Figure 11
Performance in examination problems, 1971-78. Area of the circle represents percentage problems in examination, shadings represent percentage of students failing (<50%) and percentage of students with mastery (80%) for the problems used from 1971-73, and from 1974 (see text).

Mastery/Failure in Individual Problems

Retention of some problems throughout this period has allowed comparison of performance between years on individual questions. The general policy was to discontinue some questions after two or more years and introduce new items with better discrimination. A criterion adopted for discontinuance of a problem question was when approximately two-thirds of the students attained mastery in it; this appeared to be maximal for the student samples under investigation. Minor changes to individual questions made over the years slightly increased the degree of difficulty without altering the basic problem.

Performance in Problem-solving Questions		Percentage of Students at Mastery (80%) and Fail (<50%)			
		1974	1975	1976	1977
		n=105	n=115	n=71	n=76
Q1	Mastery	39	68	*N/A	N/A
	Fail	12	5	N/A	N/A
Q2	Mastery	18	69	(65)	68
	Fail	33	12	(13)	9
Q3	Mastery	11	17	(19)	33
	Fail	35	28	(29)	15
Q4	Mastery	*N/A	40	(37)	61
	Fail	N/A	19	(21)	8
Q5	Mastery	*N/A	36	(31)	52
	Fail	N/A	41	(38)	29

*Not applicable: question not used until 1975, or discontinued from 1976.

Table 8
Percentage of students gaining mastery (80% or >) and failing (<50%) in scores for five individual examination problem questions in the years 1974, 1975 and 1977 (cohorts of comparable ability). Results for 1976 (in brackets) show no significant change from 1975.

Table 8 presents the percentages of students gaining mastery and failing in five problems, across two or three cohorts. For reasons already indicated, relevant comparisons of performance in individual problems may be made between the cohorts of 1974, 1975 and 1977. Results for 1976 are included solely to indicate that there is no significant increase or decrease in performance levels from those attained in 1975.

In all five problems, for the cohorts of 1974/75/77, there is a significant *increase* (this chapter, Note 22) in percentage students gaining *mastery* (across 2 or 3 cohorts) accompanied by a *decrease* in the percentage students *failing*.

Question 5, introduced in 1975, and the multiple steps for its solution, are given here (this chapter, Notes 12 and 13).

CONCLUSIONS

Central to the prime problem of higher education, is the strategy to be used when students are taught how to solve problems. One common approach is to present examples of complex problems, and, when the students' skill comes to be tested, to measure achievement by their ability to solve problems analogous to the patterns of problems presented. The students' capacity to do this is thus necessarily confined to the limits of the analogy and consequently is assumed by some to be incapable of expansion. Another approach – and the one adopted in SIMIG – differs basically from this common approach, for it presents (in the discussion groups), not examples of *complex* problems, but the separate skills and strategies required in their solution, together with limited practice in *simple* problems requiring about three operational steps. Although students' ability to transfer these individual skills and strategies (learned in interactive peer groups) to complex problems is not tested until the final examination at the end of the course, a surprisingly high percentage of students have demonstrated their ability to do so.

Negatively skewed distribution of examination scores is characteristic of the notion of mastery learning (Bloom 1968; Block 1971). A performance level of 80% was chosen as a realistic definition of mastery of content for the anatomy course. Students were encouraged to attain mastery, but existing constraints precluded 'enforcement', as in other methods based on mastery learning, eg the Keller Plan (1968). Nonetheless, the negatively skewed frequency distribution typical of the SIMIG courses inevitably produced difficulties, for academics commonly subscribe to a belief that examination scores should by some sort of natural law fall on a symmetrical, normal distribution curve. It was not surprising, therefore, that some of my colleagues in other departments assumed – at least in the early years of the SIMIG experiment – that either my course must present no serious challenge to students, or the marking was too 'soft'.

In my view this expectation that examination scores should fall on a normal distribution curve is misguided, not to say pernicious. Normality is what one naturally expects from randomness, eg from measurements of the heights of male adults in a population uniform in race and living conditions. But as soon as any kind of selection is made (eg exclusion of men below a certain height in recruitment for the police, or the inclusion of a large percentage of jockeys or coxswains of racing boats) the curve becomes skewed. It is a sign that something has acted upon a population which would otherwise have been randomly distributed. This is precisely what does happen to samples of persons selected or trained to get high scores in examinations. In an élite university, or in élite faculties, eg Medicine in Sydney, where there is strong competition for entry, the capacity to get high scores would be expected to produce negatively skewed curves even without any subsequent differential effects of teaching. In the School of Biological Sciences at Sydney this may not have been the case, but there is no reason whatever to doubt that some strategies of teaching, designed to increase the chances of a mediocre student to get a high mark, would produce distribution curves of examination scores different in shape from those produced by strategies of teaching designed to sort out – and keep sorted out – the best from the mediocre students. This, in my view, is precisely the reason why the distribution curves for those taught by SIMIG differ from the curves of the very same students taught in other courses by other strategies. I believe that the statistical analysis supports this view and eliminates the two assumptions made by some of my colleagues as mentioned at the end of the last paragraph.

For the university teacher, the paramount question to be answered is: does the SIMIG method increase the number of students in the class who will have achieved what Bloom calls mastery of the content of the course? In the language of statistics, this becomes: is the distribution curve of marks in the final examination skewed in the direction of better performance if students have learnt by the SIMIG method instead of by conventional methods? The answer to this question is indubitably 'yes'.

NOTES 9-22

9   In Table 2 probability values varied from <0.02 to <0.001.

10 The reliability of the examination (calculated by the Kuder Richardson$_{21}$ formula) over the last five years was high and always greater than 0.8 (eg $KR_{21} \sim 0.9$ in 1977). Content validity also has been high, analysed in respect of specific objectives for each study module.

11 In Table 5 the average increase per year in percentage pass rate, calculated as a weighted (to allow for varying numbers per year) linear regression coefficient of percentage passing on year, is significantly greater than zero for questions 4-7. (z is the standard normal variate, calculated as $\dfrac{\text{regression coefficient}}{\text{standard error}}$

The values obtained were:
Question 4: $z = 2.34$, $P<0.05$
Question 5: $z = 4.35$, $P<0.001$
Question 6: $z = 4.45$, $P<0.001$
Question 7: $z = 7.45$, $P<0.001$

12 *Problem question used in examination 1975 to 1977* (Q 5 in Table 8)
Based on Module 1, with some reference to Module 9.
Material Transverse sections of leaves (slides 1 to 5).
Answer parts (a) and (c)

(a) Indicate the anatomy of each leaf in terms of the type of pathway of carbon assimilation (C_3 or C_4), and any anatomical features (other than Kranz or non-Kranz) which may be used to clarify the explanation (reasons) in part (c).

(b) In duplicate experiments, leaves of five plants (K-O) were exposed to radioactive $^{14}CO_2$ in the light and in the dark for 30 seconds. Results of incorporation of radioactive carbon are expressed as CPM/gm.f.wt. (radioactivity in counts per minute per gram fresh weight), for both the total incorporation of carbon (C) and carbon into organic acids.
Results are tabled below:

Leaves of Plants	Total Incorporation of C		Incorporation of C in Organic Acids	
	Light	Dark	Light	Dark
K	9000	69	8100	65
L	7250	77	6320	70
M	5470	114	832	110
N	4990	108	790	105
O	4130	4710	1050	3240

(c) Match the leaf sections (by slide number) which would be most likely to give patterns of labelling tabled in (b). Briefly indicate your reasons, referring to the anatomical features listed in section (a).

Part a: Of the five leaf sections, only one had been seen previously.

Part b: Data of this type were entirely unfamiliar.

Part c: No previous experience.

13   *Analysis of steps required to solve problem in Note 12*

Several days after the 1977 examination eight of the best students were asked (individually) to recall their strategies for working through this problem. The majority followed the sequence of steps outlined below and categorized as 'skills'.

Part a : 4 out of 5 sections previously unseen

1   *Recall and comprehension (from Module 1)* of the two basic patterns of leaf structure (Kranz and non-Kranz) and their associated biochemical pathways (C4 and C3 respectively) of carbon assimilation.

2   *Application* of the above to the five leaf sections, for the following decisions:
   – slides 1 & 3 (Kranz) – C4; slides 2 & 5 (non-Kranz) – C 3
   – slide 4 (non-Kranz) – C3 (and perhaps CAM?) a variation of C 3 (from Module 9)

'Other anatomical features' might be added now or deferred until Part c

Part b : Data unfamiliar in format and content

3   *Comprehension and application (from Modules 1 and 9)* of the following to data presented in the table in Part b.
   – C4 plants incorporate carbon predominantly into organic acids in the light while C3 plants do not.
   – C4 plants usually incorporate more carbon in the light than C3 plants.
   – CAM plants incorporate C both in light and dark, but in the dark, C is preferentially incorporated in organic acids.

4   *Analysis* of the table to select the following leaves of plants:
   K & L: similar rates of C incorporation of C4 type.
   M & N: similar rates of C incorporation of C3 type.
   O: one example of C incorporation of CAM type.

Part c

5   *Synthesis* in combining this selected information from Parts a and b:
   – slides 1 & 3 with leaves K & L : C4; slides 2 & 5 with leaves M & N : C3; slide 4 with leaf O : CAM

6   *Evaluation* is required to make the judgement between the two pairs of C4 and C3 leaf types, based on anatomical features and physiological data. The 'other anatomical features' first observed in Part a must now be critically evaluated, and used to match leaves of plants with slide sections: K = 1, L = 3, M = 5, N = 2.

14   The most probable explanation for the increase in mastery level from 1968 to 1969 and 1970 appears to be the changeover from traditional teaching methods to self-instruction, as the percentage marks awarded to application/comprehension questions were increased (Fig. 3), and it has been demonstrated (Table 5) that students found these to be more difficult than recall of knowledge items.

15   Introduction of problem-solving questions in the 1971 examination

revealed a decline in mean class score and in performance at mastery level (Table 6 and Fig. 4), resulting from poor performance in problem questions. As already noted, in one problem (Question 7, Table 5), whereas the failure rate was 74 per cent in 1971, the pass rate in 1972 was 75 per cent. The most probable explanation for this appears to be that, previous to the introduction in 1972 of the new style of group discussions associated with slide projections, students were not practising the skills necessary for solving problems in examination.

16 The frequency distributions were less skewed in 1973 and 1974 than in 1975, and fewer students attained mastery level than in the preceding (1972) and subsequent years (Table 6). During this period, 1973-74, the difficulty of the examination had been increased by:

    a 17 to 20 per cent more problem questions than in 1972 (Fig. 4).

    b Replacement in 1974 of most of the problems used in the earlier examinations by more demanding ones.

It is also presumed that the 1975 cohort benefited from the complete revision of group discussion questions for that year.

17 As already noted, the 1976 and 1978 cohorts were shown to be below the calibre of the 1975 and 1977 cohorts, as judged by three tests (Table 2). So, for the 1976 cohort to maintain performance at the 1975 level was better than might have been expected. Other factors must therefore be the cause of the marked improvement in performance of the 1978 cohort − of comparable ability to the 1976 cohort. Evidence presented in Chapter 5 (Note 27) suggests that this improvement in performance of the 1978 class is attributable to improvements in group techniques.

18 $z = 0.66, P<0.0001$.

19 Performance (as percentages ± standard error) in the two categories of questions used in examination for the 1974, 1975 and 1977 cohorts (of comparable ability):

Categories of Questions	1974		Percentages ± S E 1975		1977
	n=105 60% Problems in Examination		n=115 69% Problems in Examination		n=76 76% Problems in Examination
Problems (P)	60.0 ± 1.45		67.3 ± 1.53		75.2 ± 1.81
		(t=3.99, P<0.001)		(t=4.07, P<0.001)	
Application/ Comprehension A/C	76.8 ± 1.66		73.7 ± 2.31		71.3 ± 3.02
		(t=1.56, NS)		(t=1.19, NS)	
Within years*	z=8.19 (P<0.001)		z=6.74 (P<0.001)		(z=1.49, NS)

*Between years, differences in the same categories were evaluated using the 't' statistic. Within years, the significance of the difference (z values) between A/C and P questions was calculated by the Wilcoxon Matched Pairs Signed Rank Test.

Mean scores for problem questions were lower than those for application/comprehension questions in 1974/75 (as they were also for 1976). *Within these years* the differences between application/comprehension and problem-solving questions were significantly different (P<0.001), ie problem questions were more difficult than application/comprehension questions. *Between years* there was a highly significant (P<0.001) difference between the problem-solving scores, but no difference between the application/comprehension scores. Thus there has been an *improvement in performance in problem-solving questions across the years 1974/77, so that in 1977 there was no longer a significant difference between scores in the two types of question.* But, with the 1978 cohort, a significant difference was again evident between percentage scores gained in problem solving (70.4%) and application/ comprehension questions (82.5%); ie for the 1978 students, problem questions were again more difficult. (Although the same basic problems were used in 1978 as for 1977, the difficulty of some problems had been increased slightly.) This result was not unexpected, considering the difference in ability at course entry between the 1977 and 1978 cohorts.

20   These can be related to specific changes in group teaching and learning strategies (see Chapter 5), notwithstanding the overall increase in complexity, number of questions and proportion of marks awarded to problem questions in examination.

21   Percentage of students gaining mastery (80%) and failing (<50%) in overall score for examination problem questions in the years 1974, 1975 and 1977 (comparable cohorts):

Level of Performance in Examination Problems	1974		Percentage of Students 1975		1977
	n=105		n=115		n=76
Overall mastery	2		17		46
(80% or >)		(z^*=3.65, P<0.001)		(z=4.33, P<0.001)	
Failure <50%	20		14		4
		(z=1.08, NS)		(z=2.24, P<0.05)	

*The z statistic and probability values are shown between pairs (ie 1974-1975; 1975-1977).

The percentage of students gaining mastery, not in all problem questions, but in a majority of questions (ie 3 our of 4 in 1974; 4 or 5 out of 6 in 1975/77) also showed a highly significant improvement (from 8 per cent in 1974, to 23 per cent in 1975, and 52 per cent in 1977; 1974/75, P<0.002 and in 1975/77, P<0.00l). A decrease in the percentage of students failing problems has accompanied this highly significant increase in mastery; the reduction is not statistically significant between 1974/75, but is significant from 1975/77 (P<0.05).

22   Percentage of students gaining mastery (80%) and failing (<50%) in five examination problem questions in the years 1974, 1975 and 1977 (cohorts of comparable ability):

Performance in Problem-solving Questions		1974		Percentage of Students 1975		1977
		n=105		n=115		n=76
Q1	Mastery	39		68		N/A
			(z=4.28, P<0.001)			
	Fail	12		5		N/A
			(z=1.84, NS)			
Q2	Mastery	18		69		68
			(z=8.79, P<0.001)		(z=0.13, NS)	
	Fail	33		12		9
			(z=3.73, P<0.001)		(z=0.65, NS)	
Q3	Mastery	11		17		33
			(z=1.25, NS)		(z=2.56, P<0.01)	
	Fail	35		28		15
			(z=1.12, NS)		(z=1.92, P~0.05)	
				(1974-7, =3.01,P<0.01)		

Performance in Problem-solving Questions		1974	Percentage of Students 1975	1977
Q4	Mastery	N/A	40	61
			$(z=2.83, P<0.01)$	
	Fail	N/A	19	8
			$(z=1.75, NS)$	
Q5	Mastery	N/A	36	52
			$(z=2.17, P<0.05)$	
	Fail	N/A	41	29
			$(z=1.69, NS)$	

5 Factors Influencing Performance in Final Examinations

In Chapter 4 it was demonstrated that over the years 1971-78 there was an overall improvement in performance in the final examination, not simply in a gradually increased command of problem-solving skills but in the attainment of mastery levels of competence in these skills. The problem to which I turned attention next was accordingly the source of these improvements. Since the self-instructional modules were designed primarily to enable students to acquire the basic material of the subject, ie the basic facts, the basic skills in observation and discrimination, and the basic concepts, I focused my inquiry at this stage on the changes in my organization of the work in the discussion groups.

CHANGES IN THE ORGANIZATION OF GROUP DISCUSSIONS

Several hypotheses offered themselves: the operative factors in the group discussions were: (i) the number of slides shown; (ii) the number of items in the categories of comprehension, application and simple (three or four step) problems; (iii) the sequencing of these three categories; (iv) the repetition of questions reinforcing the same concept, sometimes with a different cognitive demand, always with different examples (slides); (v) the length of the discussion periods; (vi) the improved skills of the tutors; (vii) the improved skills of the students in the interaction within the groups; (viii) an increase in the strength of motivation generated in the groups. Various sets of data accumulated over the eight-year period were analysed.

Performance in Three Examination Problems 1974, 1975 and 1977

The records of group discussion materials used in the above years were analysed in relation to student performance in three of the final examination questions set in those years. The results are shown in Table 9.

The improvement in performance at mastery level in Question 1, from 1974 to 1975, appears to be quite clearly associated with an increase in the number of slides (visual examples shown in the groups) that had a bearing on the skills involved.

For Question 3, an increase in the number of slides used in groups in 1975 appears to have had no statistically significant influence on the improvement of scores at mastery level between 1974 and 1975. But there is a statistically significant improvement in performance between 1975 and 1977, when the number of application and problem-solving questions used with these slides was doubled.

Problem Question from Table 8	Media Variables used in Groups	Years			Variable(s) most likely to have been Effective in Improved Performance
		1974	1975	1977	
Q1	% students 80% or >	39*	68*	–	
	No. of slides	10	16		Increase in no. of slides
	C,A,P test items		no change		
Q3	% students 80% or >	11	17*	33*	74/75 Increase in slides
	No. of slides	8	16	16	No significant effect
	A + P test items	2	3	6	75/77 Increase in no. and cognitive demand of test items associated with slides
Q5	% students 80% or >		36*	52*	
	No. of slides		4	15	Increase in no. of slides
	C test items		2	2	and no. of (A) test items
	A test items		2	6	(See also Note 23)
	P test items		0	0	

*Significant change in performance between pairs of cohorts 1974/1975, and 1975/1977. For probability (P) values between years, see Note 22.

Table 9
Variables used in groups (increase in cognitive demand of test items and/or number of slide transparencies) most likely to have been effective in a significant improvement in performance at mastery level (80%) or more in three problems (from Table 8) used in final examination for two or more successive years from 1974 to 1977. Abbreviations for categories of test items: C = comprehension, A= application, P = problem.

With regard to Question 5, there appears to be a correlation between the significant improvement in performance from 1975 to 1977 and (a) the number of slides used, (b) the number of application questions, and also (c) repetition (to reinforce a particular concept, using different slides and types of application questions; see Chapter 3, Note 6 and this chapter, Note 23).

Performance in One Examination Problem 1971-1977
One question (this chapter, Note 24) was retained throughout the period and Figure 12 shows the shift in frequency distribution of performance levels over these years. The fall in the percentage of failures and the first achievement of mastery level in 1972 coincide with the introduction of the slide-based group work (see p. 48). There is clear-cut evidence to confirm hypothesis (i) of those listed above (p. 60) for the sequence of results from 1974 to 1975 and in the two subsequent years. In 1974 twelve additional slides were added, of which four were highly relevant to the examination problem as they were examples of a particular tissue, the recognition of which was essential to final solution of the problem. In 1975 I omitted these four slides from the group discussions and reinstated them in 1976 and 1977 (Table 1).

Figure 12 shows that the examination results in 1975 were adversely affected, although performance in all other problems during the years 1974 and 1975 increased, most of them significantly (Chapter 4, Note 22). As is shown in Note 25 (this chapter) the difference between the percentages of mastery performances is statistically significant at 0.1 per cent level. In 1976 and 1977 the performance levels returned to the pattern established in 1974. It seems clear that the four extra slides in the discussion groups provided a reinforcement or extension of the learning acquired in the self-instructional modules (where the relevant tissue was examined).

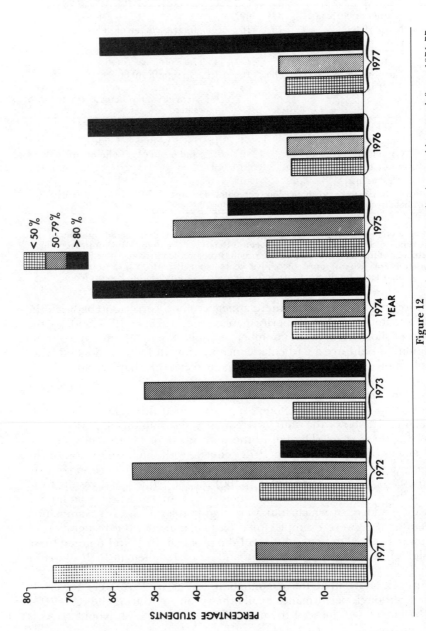

Figure 12

Relative frequency distribution of scores at three performance levels in one examination problem used from 1971-77. Slide-based group work, introduced in 1972, coincided with the first achievement of mastery level for this problem. In 1974, four extra slides (relevant to solution of the problem) were used in group discussions, removed in 1975, and re-instated in 1976/77. This experiment reduced the mastery level in 1975.

Analysis of the marks scored in 1975 for different parts of this question (this chapter, Note 25) reveals the interesting evidence that students' ability to analyse the problem from the data presented was not adversely affected. The distribution of marks showed that 77 per cent had correctly interpreted and evaluated the data, but only 32 per cent had *observed and recognized the particular tissue* in the specimen provided, which allowed the accomplishment of the final step.

Phases of Accelerated Improvement in Performance 1971-78

As already noted in Chapter 4 (Fig. 4 and p. 44; Fig. 11 and p. 51) there were certain periods in which performance levels rose particularly steeply, namely 1971-72, 1974-75 and 1975-77. These phases coincided with fresh developments in the group work, as already reported in Chapter 3. In 1972 the slide-based discussion groups were introduced (p. 24) and my subjective impression at the time was that the presentation of the visual material as a basis of discussion not only improved comprehension but also greatly enlivened the debate.

In 1974-75 the proportions of test items used in the groups, in the more demanding categories − of application and problem-solving − were doubled and trebled respectively (Fig. 1 and p. 29). In addition, the test items were revised and re-designed to improve their discriminative capacity. This development was prompted by the disappointing level of performance in 1973 and 1974, when overall performance at mastery level dropped to less than half of that in 1972 (Fig. 4) and only 2 per cent attained mastery in problem questions (Fig. 11). It was evident that the discussion groups were not providing the experience in higher order skills to enable average students to cope with an examination in which, by 1974, problem questions constituted 60% of the total marks.

Between 1975 and 1977 there was a further increase in the proportion of higher-category items (Fig. 1) and there was a steep rise in the number of slides used in the discussion sessions (Table 1 and p. 29). At this stage also the discussion periods were lengthened: to one and a half hours in 1976 and to two hours in 1978.

Sequencing of Material

My subjective impression is that by careful sequencing of questions I have enabled students to incorporate new material and concepts into those already established (Bruner 1966; Ausubel 1968). I have been unable to obtain any objective evidence to show that the sequencing of questions in group discussions affects learning. The pattern of presentation used in group test papers (see Chapter 3, Note 5) does appear to alleviate the build up of anxiety that many students experience.

Improved Tutor Skills

My colleagues and I believed that we became more adept at this style of work over the years. There was no staff training in group work, but before taking their own groups new tutors were invited to observe the techniques used in group discussions. Some evidence of the effect of tutor's skills on student performance is presented in Chapter 7 (p. 96).

Improved Student Skills
A comparison of Notes 7 and 8 (in Chapter 3) giving excerpts from peer discussion (with the same nine students) in the first and last groups, shows that the skills of interaction have, indeed, improved over the eight weeks.

Increase in Motivation
There was a marked improvement in the percentage of students achieving mastery level in continuing assessment tests over the period 1974 to 1977: from 11 per cent in 1974, to 22 per cent in 1975, to 36 per cent in 1977. In each cohort from 1975 to 1978, mediocre students, classified as Type III (p. 88) also showed a marked improvement over weeks in scores for continuing assessment (Fig. 18). It has also been demonstrated that during this period, the distribution of weekly test scores changed from normal to skewed by the fifth week (Fig. 13). All these observations could be interpreted as reflecting increased motivation generated in the groups by an improvement in group process over both weeks and years.

It is generally conceded that successful performance and continued improvement generate motivation: students become interested in and 'like' a subject because they perceive themselves to be learning meaningfully, as with those Type III students who have attributed their success to effective group work (Chapter 8, p. 109).

Thus it appears that most of the hypotheses are supported; some more strongly than others.

CHANGES IN THE ORGANIZATION OF THE SELF-INSTRUCTIONAL WORK
It also seemed advisable to check the available evidence on the self-instructional work, in relation to two hypotheses: (i) that the improved results were due to an increase in the time spent on private study of the modules; and (ii) that they were due to substantial revision of the self-instructional materials.

Time spent on Self-instruction
Table 10 shows the number of hours spent by students on the self-instructional modules and achievement in examination in five grades. It is clear that over the period 1975-78 there was no increase in time spent on self-instruction; in fact from 1975 to 1978 students achieving mastery spent less time on it. Certain other aspects are of interest.

First, over the whole sample (n = 317) the difference between the mean time spent by students attaining mastery and the means of all other grades is statistically significant (P<0.01, Table 10).

Second, this relationship between mastery and time spent is by no means universal: the records show that some individuals in each cohort who attained mastery spent up to eight hours per week in the learning centre (investigating optional material) and a few (with ability but no particular interest in the subject) completed the modules in four hours. This not only provides evidence in favour of self-paced study, but also that attainment of mastery level by *individual* students is not determined by time. The overall significant relationship between mastery in examination and time spent on self-instruction may be interpreted as an example of the generally accepted

Year (n)	Time Spent (hours) and Examination Scores					Correlations – Average Time: Exam Score
	Mastery 100-80%	79-70%	69-60%	59-50%	Fail 50%	
1975 (110)	6.2	5.1	4.8	4.8	4.5	0.34
1976 (72)	6.0	5.7	5.5	5.3	5.7	0.15
1977 (73)	5.7	5.2	5.1	4.7	4.3	0.27
1978 (62)	5.0	5.3	4.8	5.2	N/A	0.05
Means (317)	5.6*	5.3*	5.1	5.0	4.9	

*The difference between times in mastery/credit grades using the 't' test = 2.61 (P<0.01).

Table 10

Mean time (hours) spent in module study and mean examination scores in five grades over four years from 1975 to 1978. The grades correspond to performance groupings of distinction, credit, pass, marginal pass and failure. Correlations are shown for average time spent: examination score in the four years. N/A = not available (ie students who failed did not have complete time records).

view that time invested in study is more a reflection of the type of student than anything else: irrespective of teaching technique, the best students usually spend more time in the study of any subject than students achieving lower grades.

Finally, as would be expected from the data presented in Table 10, the correlations between average time spent in independent module study with performance in final examination for each year were higher in 1975 and 1977 than in 1976 and 1978. These statistics may be related in some way to the difference in ability between these comparable pairs of cohorts.

Revision of the Self-instructional Materials

There was a quite substantial revision of the study guide and most of the audiotapes for the 1975 edition. This may have contributed to the improvement of results in 1975. No further substantial revision was carried out during the period under review, although there was a revised edition of the study guide in 1977.

MANIPULATIVE SKILLS TEST

This test (described in Appendix A: Records and Tests) indicated students' ability to prepare slides of plant material for microscopic examination. They were used continually in course work, and in examination. Lack of expertise in this skill could adversely affect performance in those problem questions which required matching of the data presented with specific tissues in the hand-cut sections. One of the hand-sections in the 1977 examination (scored for manipulative skills test No. 2) predicted outcome for all problem questions in examination (P<0.01).

Although preparation of sections is not taught in the modules, explicit directions are given in the study guide. Students who initially experience difficulty in this skill are advised to seek help from the demonstrator.

CONCLUSIONS

The improvements made each year, especially from 1975, to teaching and learning strategies in group discussions, which may have sharpened the skills that students require for solving anatomical problems, are summarized below.

The revision, for the 1975 cohort, of questions — by item analysis — improved discrimination; while the design of a pattern of presentation of items for discussion provided a suitable sequence of ease and difficulty of cognitive demand. With the extension of time in group sessions to one and a half hours in 1976/77, and to two hours in 1978, there was more time for peer discussion in relation to time spent on written responses to test items. Tutors also became more adept in the role of stimulating discussion and group process improved with time. As a consequence there was an increase in the strength of motivation generated in the groups and a greater commitment to study. More effective use of media resulted from the yearly increase in quality and quantity of visual examples (slide transparencies). These were made especially to broaden students' familiarity with biological variation, and to provide opportunities for practising their skills of application to previously unseen material. Increases in the number of slide transparencies allowed concurrent increases, over the years, in the proportion of items testing higher cognitive skills. Consequently more time was spent on discussion of difficult aspects, which not only enlivened the debate, but provided for some students fresh insight into the ways in which their peers approached a problem.

NOTES 23 - 25

23 An increase of application test items from 2 in 1975 to 6 in 1977 was made possible by four additional transparencies.

All six application tests reinforced the concepts of C3 and C4 leaf anatomy. They were spaced in pairs at intervals during the 1½ hours of the group discussion. Transfer of learning resulted from this technique of repetition: the percentages of correct responses increased across all groups (n = 76) from 53% to 93% (see Chapter 3, Note 6).

To solve this examination problem (Question 5, in Note 12) the first essential step was the transfer of this type of information from previously unseen examples (microscope slides) to 'Part a' of the problem. The operational steps required to solve this problem are given in Chapter 4, Note 13.

24 *Problem-solving question used in examinations 1971 to 1977*
This question (based on Modules 2 and 4) was retained in exactly the same format (given below) from 1974 to 1976, ie prior to and immediately after the 'critical' experiment in 1975. A simpler version was used from 1971 to 1973. In 1977, although the same data were presented, two specimens had to be identified. This problem was set again in 1978, but with three specimens and a format which precluded comparison with previous years (manipulative skills test no. 2 — see Appendix A: Records and Tests).

A suitably replicated experiment was carried out as follows:
$^{14}CO_2$ was given to the photosynthesizing leaves of two species of plants in the light; large quantities of radioactive CO_2 were taken up. Half of the plants of both species were ringed (ie tissue removed down to the vascular cambium). After 24 hours the roots and stems of all plants were ground up and total radioactivity of each measured. Results of ^{14}C activity are tabled below as CPM/gm.F.wt. (counts per

min per gm fresh weight):

		Species 1*	Species 2
Intact plants	(stem)	6300	3000
	(root)	900	400
Ringed plants	(stem above ring)	5800	4100
	(root & stem below ring)	–	250

*Species 1 assimilated C at a faster rate than Species 2.

a. Specimen F is a piece of one of the stems. Identify specimen F as species 1 or species 2, giving your reason(s).
b. Support your diagnosis by a map diagram of a small sector of the stem, labelling features which you used for identification of specimen F.

Attach a label provided to the slide prepared from specimen H.

NB You will not be marked for the quality of the section.

25 Performance of candidates in three categories of marks scored in a problem question in successive years from 1971-1977. Mastery level: 80%; failure: <50%:

% exam marks	1971[1]	1972	1973	1974[2]	1975[3]	1976	1977[1]
	n=119	n=108	n=94	n=105	n=115	n=71	n=76
< 50	74	25	17	17	23	17	18
50-79	26	55	52	19	45	18	20
80-100	–	20	31	64	32	65	62

[1] 1971-1974 $\big\{$ average increase per year gaining 80% or >. $z=10.65$ (P<0.001)

[2] 1974/75 $\quad x^2=15.49$ (P<0.001)

[3] Variation of treatment in groups in 1975, with omission of four slide transparencies in groups (reinforcing a particular anatomical feature essential to solution of problem).

[4] In 1977 (but not in 1976, with a less competent cohort), an increase in examination performance may have been expected, but an addition to this question in 1977 (see introduction to Note 24 in this chapter) could have masked any additional improvement.

6 Methods of Assessment: 2 Weekly Tests

As has already been explained, the group discussion techniques underwent a long evolutionary process. From 1969 to 1971 there were no seminar rooms that could be used for the projection of slides. Various experiments were tried: with microscopes furnished with identical slides and with xeroxed diagrams; but these were unsatisfactory. Weekly tests were a part of the programme in the group meetings from the outset, but they constituted 15% only of the overall course assessment during 1969-71. Over this period about fourteen group sessions of one hour per week were scheduled for approximately 120 students.

A purpose-built seminar room was secured in 1972 and by this time, with the assistance of the departmental photographer and a technician skilled in photomicrography, I had assembled a small bank of transparencies (this chapter, Note 26) of anatomical sections. Questions were formulated around these for use in the groups.

As noted previously (p. 25) test items, which required a written answer, were scored for assessment with answers scoring either 0 or 1 mark per question, irrespective of the level of cognitive demand. Although there was a rigorous marking system, credit had always been given for reasonable student responses, not necessarily for one 'right' answer. Reliability (ie consistency) of the weekly tests was high (KR = 0.70), especially as many objectives were tested within each session.

Average scores for the group and the whole cohort during the previous week were always announced at the beginning of each group session, when marked papers were returned individually to group members. This stimulated many students whose scores were below average to improve their performance. As from 1972 the weekly test scores accounted for half of the overall assessment in this course; failure in a weekly test was an additional incentive to perform better in subsequent group meetings. Nevertheless, emphasis was placed on learning by discussion, not by competition. The pattern of the test paper (described on p. 26) ensured a suitable sequence of ease and difficulty of items, with 'discussion only' questions at intervals to alleviate the build-up of stress for anxious students.

Retrospective analysis of tests prior to 1975 was impossible as, unlike examination scripts, marked test papers were returned to students each week. It was only from 1975 to 1978 (for the project on learning profiles) that detailed records were kept for each student of scores in the four cognitive categories of test items. For this period only can comparisons of performance in weekly tests be presented. Of the eight assessment tests given during the nine-week course, the first six modules only were used in the detailed analysis of performance and the concurrent analysis of time spent in independent study modules. These were the only records strictly comparable for both performance and time (see Appendix A: Records and Tests).

The following aspects were studied: (1) *change over six weeks in* mean performance of cohorts over four years, frequency distributions of cohorts by grades, frequency distributions of cohorts, graphs of raw scores; (2) *correlation of performance with* changes in content of group discussion, time spent on independent study of modules; (3) *relation between* level of performance of group and that of individual members, individual performance and field-dependence or field-independence.

ANALYSIS OF PERFORMANCE IN SIX WEEKLY TESTS 1975-78
Change in Mean Performance of Cohorts over Four Years
Table 11 shows the mean performance (as percentages) in six tests on modules over six weeks during the four years of investigation (1975 to 1978). It is apparent that an increase in performance of approximately 10 per cent occurs over the weekly tests, within each year.

Between years, mean performances were significantly different (this chapter, Note 27) and higher in 1975 and 1977, again reflecting the different calibre of the pairs of cohorts 1975/77 and 1976/78 (see Table 2).

Modules/ Weeks	Mean Performance (as percentages) in Modules				Mean Performance/ Modules
	1975	1976	1977	1978	
	n=115	n=70	n=75	n=62	
1	66	61	68	63	66
2	64	61	70	58	65
3	71	65	72	65	70
4	77	67	71	65	72
5	72	65	74	67	71
6	73	70	77	72	75
Mean/Year	71	65	72	65	

Table 11
Mean performance in six weekly tests on six modules in four successive years 1975-78. Results are expressed as percentages (to nearest whole number). For standard errors of performance and statistics on difference in performance between years, see Note 27 in this chapter.

Change in Frequency Distributions of Cohorts: by Grades
Further information about the 10 per cent improvement over the six-week period emerges from the distribution of students, at five grade levels, for each of the six modules. (Grades were not given to students, they are used here only for analysis of results.) Three sets of frequency distributions (as percentage scores) are given (Table 12, A, B, C).

From the analysis over four years (1975-78) it is evident that percentages of students scoring more than 70% increase with time; the percentage in the two grades 60 - 69 and 50 - 59 remain fairly constant while — and this is the interesting point — the percentage who fail drops dramatically. Within this

Modules/ weeks (n)	Percentage Distribution in Grades				
	Mastery 100-80%	79-70%	69-60%	59-50%	Fail <50%
A　1975-1978					
1　(311)	13	28	35	15	9
2　(309)	13	31	30	18	8
3　(307)	17	33	30	18	2
4　(298)	16	37	33	11	3
5　(301)	18	35	30	13	4
6　(317)	21	35	30	12	2
Means	16	33	31	15	5
B　1976					
1　(70)	7	19	45	16	13
2　(69)	4	25	36	25	10
3　(68)	10	30	34	23	3
4　(65)	12	34	32	14	8
5　(68)	14	29	37	13	7
6　(69)	17	43	28	12	0
Means	11	30	35	17	7
C　1978					
1　(62)	16	16	29	21	18
2　(59)	19	17	22	29	13
3　(62)	23	10	26	27	14
4　(62)	17	14	32	26	11
5　(60)	22	15	32	23	8
6　(60)	25	8	32	27	8
Means	20	13	29	26	12

Table 12
Three sets of frequency distributions of cohorts in tests on six modules over six weeks, shown as percentage of students in five grades: A The mean of four cohorts 1975 to 1978; B The 1976 cohort; C The 1978 cohort.

general pattern of distribution slight variations occur in any particular cohort (Table 12, B, C) but these do not invalidate the main conclusion. Two further points emerge:

i　The mean scores over six weeks were the same for the cohorts in 1976 and 1978 (Table 11), but the percentage achieving mastery over the six weeks was significantly different (11 per cent in 1976 and 20 per cent in 1978).

ii　Data for 1978 show a bimodal distribution of grades, absent from 1976.

Change in Frequency Distributions of Cohorts: by Raw Scores

Improvement in performance (as percentage scores) over the six weeks analysed has already been demonstrated (Tables 11 and 12). Raw scores, ie the actual marks gained in 24 test items per week for 1976 and 16 items per week for 1978, are used in the graphs (Figs. 13 and 14). These show the changes in frequency distribution of students in test scores over six weeks for the 1976 and 1978 cohorts.

In 1976 (Fig. 13) frequency distributions changed from 'normal' (Weeks 1 to 3), to a slight negative skew (Week 4) and to markedly skewed (Weeks 5

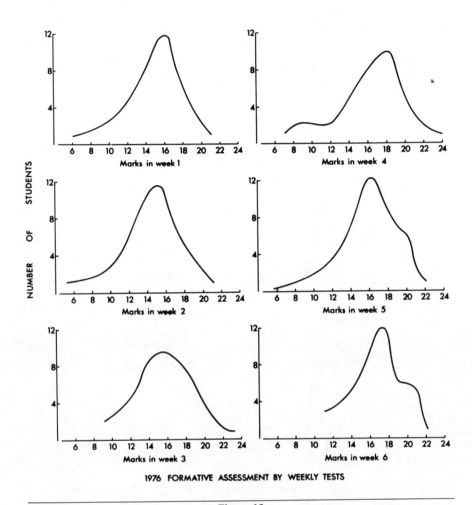

1976 FORMATIVE ASSESSMENT BY WEEKLY TESTS

Figure 13
Frequency distribution of scores for the first six weeks of tests on Modules 1 to 6 in 1976 (n=71). The curves of closest fit were obtained by plotting the number of students against the actual marks gained in 24 test items per week (8 in recall of knowledge, 5 in comprehension, 6 in application and 5 in problems). Frequency distributions changed from 'normal' (Weeks 1 to 3), to a slight negative skew (Week 4) and to markedly skewed (Weeks 5 and 6).

and 6). Similar distributions were characteristic of the 1977 cohort (see Fig. 18).

The interesting feature in the frequency distributions for 1978 (Fig. 14) is the bimodal curve (not apparent in other years) which emerged in the second week and changed gradually to a negative skew with a double peak. By the sixth week the distribution approximated the type of bimodality graphed (Fig. 9) for the 1978 final examination, with the higher peak (ie higher frequencies) in the middle range of the distribution. In 1978, bimodal curves in frequency distribution of weekly test scores have been disclosed by discrimination of the test items, and differential acceleration among different kinds of students.

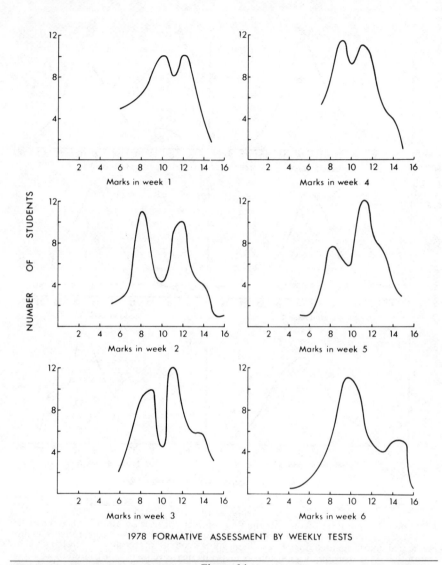

1978 FORMATIVE ASSESSMENT BY WEEKLY TESTS

Figure 14

Frequency distributions of scores for the first six weeks of tests on Modules 1 to 6 in 1978 (n=65). The curves of closest fit were obtained by plotting the number of students against the actual marks gained in 16 test items each week (four in recall of knowledge, three each in comprehension and application, and six problems). Frequency distributions were bimodal in Weeks 2 and 3, negatively skewed in Weeks 4 to 6, with 'bimodal' frequencies in Weeks 5 and 6. (Compare distribution in Week 6 with distribution in final examination Fig. 9.)

CORRELATIONS OF PERFORMANCE WITH OTHER VARIABLES

Two variables are considered: changes in the content of group discussion, and time spent on independent study of modules.

Changes in Content of Group Discussion

Changes in the quality and quantity of media used in group discussions (Table 1 and Fig. 1) have been correlated with changes in final examination scores, particularly with increases in performance at mastery level in examination problems (Table 9 and Fig. 12). The higher cognitive demand of test items over years (Fig. 1) again should be emphasized in the interpretation of changes both in mean performance in weekly tests over four years (Table 11) and in frequency distribution of scores over six successive weeks (Table 12 and Figs. 13 and 14).

As the proportion of categories of test items is approximately the same in 1975 and 1976, the lower performance levels of the 1976 cohort (Table 11) can be attributed only to the poorer average quality of the students in 1976 (Table 2). By contrast, the ability of the 1977 students was reflected by their higher performance in weekly test scores (Table 11), notwithstanding an increase of 9 per cent in the category of simple problems (Fig. 2).

In 1978 there were almost 20 per cent more problems in the tests than in 1976, but mean performance scores were the same (Table 11), although these two cohorts were judged, at entry, to be comparable in average quality. Nevertheless, the graphs of frequency distribution (Figs. 13 and 14) show that performance in weekly tests was indeed dissimilar in these two cohorts: in 1978, with six problems in a total of sixteen items, tests were more discriminative, and resulted in bimodal distributions in the first few weeks, subsequently becoming skewed and bimodal.

Time spent on Independent Study of Modules
It was shown in Chapter 5 that there was no correlation between improved performance in final examinations and length of time spent on self-instruction (Table 10). Similarly it is important to know whether the 10 per cent improvement in weekly tests on six successive modules (Table 11) is accounted for by a trend, across the six weeks of each course, for students to spend more time in independent study of modules. Table 13 shows that the average time spent on module study did not increase over the six-week period. The variations in time spent seem likely to have been caused by specific factors: the greater length of the audiotape in Module 2, the greater difficulty of the concepts in Module 5.

| Module | Mean Time Spent (hours) in Module Study 1975-78 | | | | Mean Time/ |
	1975	1976	1977	1978	Modules
	n=111	n=70	n=75	n=60	
1	5.4	5.5	5.4	5.5	5.4
2	5.7	6.2	6.0	5.8	5.9
3	4.5	4.5	4.4	4.0	4.4
4	5.0	5.1	4.4	4.7	4.8
5	5.1	5.7	5.8	5.4	5.5
6	4.5	6.3	5.5	5.5	5.3
Mean Time/ Years	5.0	5.5	5.2	5.2	

Table 13
Mean time (hours) spent in independent study of six modules (one per week) in four successive years 1975-78. For standard errors see Note 28 in this chapter.

Nonetheless, it still seemed possible that there might be a correlation between the time spent by students on module study and the scores they gained in the weekly tests.

Module		Time Spent and Performance Grades in Module Tests 1975-78									
		Mastery 80%		79-70%		69-60%		59-50%		Fail <50%	
	n	hours	n	hours	n	hours	n	hours	n	hours	n
1	311	5.8	(42)	5.3	(77)	5.5	(106)	5.3	(57)	5.3	(29)
2	309	7.0	(40)	6.1	(92)	5.9	(89)	5.5	(53)	5.5	(35)
3	307	4.7	(54)	4.4	(102)	4.4	(92)	4.2	(56)	4.7	(3)
4	298	4.9	(51)	4.8	(114)	4.9	(95)	4.8	(31)	4.0	(7)
5	301	5.8	(55)	5.5	(106)	5.5	(86)	5.2	(38)	5.3	(16)
6	317	5.3	(62)	5.6	(102)	5.0	(90)	5.3	(56)	4.6	(7)
Mean time		5.8*		5.1*		5.1		5.1		5.1	

*The difference between mean times for mastery/credit grades using the 't' test = 3.07 (P<0.01).

Table 14
Mean time (hours) spent in study of six modules and mean performance in weekly tests on modules during four successive years 1975-78. Figures in brackets indicate number of students in each grade/module. Correlations for mean time and mean performance are given in Note 29 in this chapter.

Correlations	Sample	1975	1976	1977	1978
		n=111	n=70	n=75	n=60
a Time spent: *weekly test scores	Individuals	0.06 ± 0.05	0.03 ± 0.06	0.10 ± 0.05	0.04 ± 0.06
b Time spent: **weekly test scores	Total	0.15 ± 0.05	0.12 ± 0.07	0.13 ± 0.06	0.02 ± 0.04

*Mean over all individuals in that cohort ± standard error.
**Average of the correlations of time:performance within the six modules ± standard error.

Table 15
Correlations (Pearson's) between time spent in independent study of modules with performance in weekly test scores for individual students in four cohorts 1975-78.

Analysis of mean time spent on study of six modules and mean performance (as grades) in weekly tests on modules over four years (Table 14) provides further information on time:performance.

i   Student numbers (in brackets in the table) increase markedly at mastery level and in the credit grade (70-79%), remain fairly stable in the two grades of pass and marginal pass (69-50%) and decrease markedly in the fail grade. The same trends in grade distribution over modules/weeks were evident in Table 12A,B. This again reinforces the notion that *improvement in levels of performance over modules/weeks is independent of time spent in module study*.

ii   Mean time spent in module study by students achieving mastery in weekly tests (5.8 hours) was significantly greater than in all other grades (5.1 hours). Comparable results were obtained for time spent and performance in examination (Table 10).

iii   Correlations (this chapter, Note 29) for mean time and mean performance in weekly tests on modules over four years show that there was no significant difference between time spent with successive pairs of grades, but the difference between time spent with mastery and fail grades was signficant at approximately 5 per cent level (see this chapter, Note 29).

Correlations between time spent in independent study of modules and weekly test scores were calculated, over the four years, for individual students (Table 15) by:

a   Overall assessment on the six modules.

b   Tests on six individual modules.

The following results were obtained:

a   Within all six modules in all four years, there was little correlation between time spent by individuals with individual performance. Not only was the average individual correlation low (approximately 0.05, Table 15 a), but the low standard error indicates that for a high proportion of students, *their performance in weekly tests on modules was not related to time spent in module study.*

b   Performance of cohorts in tests on modules was also independent of time spent. The correlations between weekly test scores with time spent in each corresponding self-instructional module were not only remarkably constant from 1975 to 1977, but only slightly positive, usually 0.12 - 0.15 (Table 15b). For example, correlations for six weeks in 1976 were: 0.05, 0.06, 0.18, 0.17, 0.14, 0.09 (mean 0.12, Table 15 b); in 1978 the corresponding correlations were all about zero.

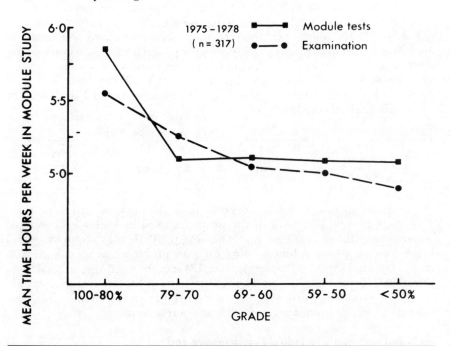

Figure 15

Mean time (hours per week) spent in module study and mean achievement over four years from 1975 to 1978 in five grades (mastery to fail) in two assessment measures: (i) tests on six modules over six weeks: (ii) in final examination.

Figure 15 graphs, for the four years from 1975 to 1978, the following:

a   Mean time spent per week on module study and mean grade achieved in weekly tests on modules (data from Table 15).

b Mean time spent and mean grade achieved in examination (data from Table 10).

Differences apparent between years — with smaller numbers and some variation in ability of cohorts — are no longer evident in the total sample (n = 317). Distribution by grades in both types of assessment is remarkably similar; the graph for overall course assessment, being equally weighted between module tests and examination, would lie between both sets of data points.

OTHER RELATIONSHIPS BETWEEN GROUP AND INDIVIDUAL PERFORMANCE

Relation between Levels of Group and Individual Performance

Kelley and Thibault (1969) delineate three possible results comparing groups versus individuals in the solving of problems: (i) groups that perform better than the best individual in the group (*synergistic*); (ii) groups that perform as well as their best individual(s) (*optimal*); and (iii) groups that perform at a lower standard than their best individual (*restricted*). While no particular research report is directly applicable to SIMIG groups — because students work first as individuals and then as a group — nonetheless some conclusions about the efficacy of SIMIG groups may be drawn from an analysis of performance on problems in groups of the 1977 cohort.

For the 1977 cohort, performance in problem questions was analysed across the seven weekly tests in all seven groups (each with an average of ten students). The results, set out below, show the number of sessions in each group where performance was better than that of the best individual (synergistic groups). In the other sessions, the groups operated at the level of the best individuals (optimal groups).

	Groups (average 10 students)						
	1	2	3	4	5	6	7
Number of synergistic group sessions (maximum 7)	4/7	5/7	6/7	4/7	4/7	5/7	3/7

Group performance was synergistic in a majority of group sessions (31/49), indicating that most of the problems used in weekly tests were of intermediate difficulty (Kelley and Thibault, p. 70), ie they required several operational steps for solution. More difficult problems, as used in SIMIG final examinations (see Chapter 4, Note 12) require many operational steps (Note 13). If these difficult problems were used in SIMIG groups, not only would the groups perform at a lower standard than their best individual, but the time available for discussion would be severely restricted.

Relation between Individual Performance and Field-dependence/independence

Another factor which affects performance relates to variation in the individual's visual skills, ie whether he is field-dependent or field-independent. Over the last twenty-five years research has suggested that there is considerable individual variation in people's ability to discriminate figure from ground. Those who can readily discern shapes within the whole are referred to as 'field-independent', whilst those who view the field as 'gestalt' or whole are called 'field-dependent' (Witkin et al. 1977). Tutors taking groups had observed that students had different capacities for distinguishing particular features in projected slides and also that adept students would respond more fluently to test items on these slides. To investigate whether these observations could be related to the dimension of field-dependence/independence, all students completed the 'hidden figures' test (see Appendix A: Records and Tests). Results obtained were compared with tutors' evaluation of behaviour in groups and students' performance in continuing and summative assessment. These results suggest the view that teaching strategies employed in the groups may compensate partially for differences in this cognitive style variable. In particular, peer discussion − after individual students have first attempted each question − is considered to be of significance. It is the field-dependent group members who appear to gain most from group discussions; they continually ask questions relating to missed cues and show improvement with time. There is some evidence that the benefit of this experience is carried over into examination questions. The correlation between the 'hidden figures' score and performance was low both in final examination (0.04) and in weekly tests (0.16). However, when results of only the top and bottom fifteen students (ie thirty) on the hidden figures test were examined, there was a significant difference (P<0.01) in correlations (0.05 cf. 0.55).

CONCLUSIONS
Analysis of weekly tests on modules for each cohort from 1975 to 1978 has shown an improvement over the nine weeks of the course. Notwithstanding differences in test scores between years, due to differences in average competence of cohorts, there is unequivocal evidence of a 10 per cent increase in overall performance across the six weekly tests for all four years reported in this study (Table 11). Moreover, the frequency distribution of these weekly test scores also changed from normal in the first week to negatively skewed by and after the fifth week (Figs. 13 and 14); more students attained mastery level and fewer failed (Table 12). This is clear evidence of the value of the modules, and more particularly of the complementary group discussions, as tools for learning, reflected by test scores throughout each course.

It has been established (Table 13) that this observed improvement was not related to an increase in time spent in self-instruction during the course. Individual improvement in levels of performance in test scores over weeks also appears to be independent of time (Table 14). There was no apparent relationship between the amount of time spent by individuals in independent study of modules and their performance outcomes (Table 15). Over the four years investigated the time : performance analyses for both weekly test scores (Table 14) and final examination (Table 10) showed a low but significant correlation between time spent and performance at mastery level in both types of assessment. Time spent in all other grades approximated to that recommended for the course (5 hours).

Self-discipline and the capacity to utilize time efficiently is of paramount importance in any method of self-instruction. A number of studies on audio-tutorial self-instruction have noted that students with complete freedom to pace themselves within the term/semester are prone to procrastinate. With self-pacing restricted to within one week for each module, and with weekly tests on modules counting 50% towards overall course assessment, this behaviour is strongly discouraged. Under these conditions it would seem that most *students invest whatever time they deem necessary to achieve an acceptable level of performance in the weekly test.*

The time taken by students to formulate a response to each item in the group sessions was such that at least half of the time spent in groups was available for peer discussion. Considerable amounts of information exchange were thus generated, particularly when the items were in the categories of application or simple problems. Peer discussion not only provided immediate feedback on each item, but more importantly catalysed effective peer learning at some time during each session for all group members. Boreham (1977) has shown also that a test's usefulness as an instructional aid is related to its position in the cognitive hierarchy; more discussion and information exchange being generated by application test items than by knowledge items.

There is little doubt that student achievement in weekly tests is a function of their varying abilities and of the extent to which they can transfer information from the study of modules to questions involving application and the solution of simple anatomical problems in groups — and subsequently to more complex ones in examination. Nevertheless, it appears reasonable to suggest that, for some individuals, the interaction apparent in 'synergistic' groups (as defined by Kelley and Thibault 1969) has improved their skills in solving problems used in weekly tests. Analysis of the teaching strategies used in groups (Chapters 3 and 5) has also shown the relative importance of the *design* and *content* of the *weekly tests*, especially in *cognitive demand* of test items, the amount of *visual exposure* to relevant material, the *sequencing* of categories of test items and the *repetition* of questions to reinforce concepts in attaining maximum examination performance in complex problems.

NOTES 26 - 29

26   From 1972 to 1975 I was building up the bank of slide transparencies. It was not until 1975 that I had a sufficient stock to be able to re-design the test items in such a way as to improve their discriminative power. Comparison of the results of student performance in 1974/75 on items requiring comprehension or application indicated that indeed the difficulty had increased ($P<0.01$). There was no difference in the performance of students on recall of knowledge items between years ($P<0.001$), but these items were significantly less demanding than items of comprehension or application within each year.

Retrospective item analysis of group tests, also in 1975, provided data for revising the tests which have been used (with some modification) since.

27   The standard errors of performance on Modules 1 to 6 (Table 11) were as follows:

        1975: ± 0.4 to ± 1.9 1976: ± 0.5 to ± 1.3

        1977: ± 0.2 to ± 1.0 1978: ± 0.6 to ± 1.8

For mean performance per year:

        1975: ± 1.1 1976: ± 0.7 1977: ± 0.4 1978: ± 1.5

and simple problem-solving. For each student, four separate graphs (this chapter, Note 30) were obtained, showing achievement from week to week in these four categories. A fifth graph ('combined skills') was drawn, in which the scores on comprehension, application and problem-solving were combined to indicate the overall development of students during the seven (Note 31) weeks of the course for which the scores were obtained. The records of performance, summarized by five separate graphs for every individual (from the four cohorts) are called *learning profiles*.

Classification as Profile Types
Learning profiles throw light upon the response of individual students to the way they are being taught. Over the four years the response of some three hundred individuals to the teaching method varied considerably. However, the variations can be summarized as four major response patterns, or *profile types*. These are called Profile Types I to IV; each type is shown in Figures 16 and 17 by one linear regression representing the *summation* of the component skills of comprehension, application and problem-solving. These four profile types (and two sub-types) were distinguished on the basis of two criteria: (1) *slope*, ie rate of change in performance with time; and (2) *intercept*, ie entry behaviour (this chapter, Notes 32 - 35).

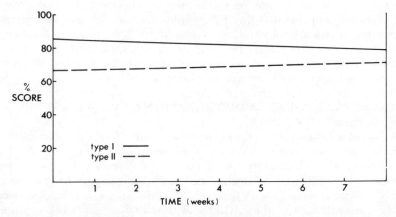

Figure 16
Profile Types I and II characterized as linear regressions of performance with time on the seven weekly tests in combined 'skills' categories of comprehension, application and problem-solving: derived from the individual profiles shown in Fig. 20.

Profiles classified as Types I and II (Fig. 16) showed no significant change in slope of the combined skills category; intercepts were used to separate them, with scores much lower in Type II. Contrastingly, Type III profiles, with two sub-types IIIA and IIIB, showed an increase in slope (steep for Type IIIA), from relatively low intercepts (Fig. 17). For students with Type IV profiles, performance deteriorated with time, although intercepts were often higher than in Type III profiles.

Thus consistently high performance levels and high entry scores (Fig. 16) characterize the brightest students with Type I profiles. Individuals with Type II profiles are average students whose initial scores are lower than those for Type I students, and whose subsequent performance is maintained

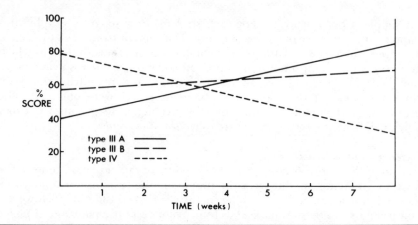

Figure 17

Profile Types IIIA, IIIB and IV characterized as linear regressions of performance with time on seven weekly tests in combined 'skills' categories of comprehension, application and problem-solving; derived from the individual profiles shown in Figs. 21 and 22.

at this lower level (Fig. 16). The Type III profile group comprise those mediocre students who are spurred on to improvement from a relatively poor performance in the first week of tests — as indicated by lower intercepts (Fig. 17). Students with Type IV profiles (~5%) fail the course, not necessarily for lack of ability.

Other parameters characterize these profile types, but first some general conclusions may be drawn from relative performance levels of the three major types in weekly tests and in final examination.

CHANGES IN FREQUENCY DISTRIBUTION OF PROFILE TYPES
Across Weeks: 1977 Cohort

It has been established (Figs. 13, 14) that the relative frequency distributions of weekly test scores in the 1976 and 1978 cohorts changed from 'normal' in the first week to negatively skewed — ie in the direction of better performance — by the fifth week. As students with Type III profiles showed the greatest improvement with time (Fig. 17), this suggested that they were largely responsible for the change in distribution of weekly scores. Confirmation was obtained by mapping, within the frequency distribution graphs of weekly scores in the first, third and fifth week (Fig. 18), the approximate range of distribution of profile types in the 1977 cohort, consisting of seventy-six students, with fifteen in Type I, nineteen in Type II, thirty-nine in Type III and three in Type IV. Distribution changed from approximately normal in the first week to negatively skewed by the fifth week. In the third week, Fig. 18 shows that some of the Type III students had shifted into the higher frequency distribution range of Type II students; by the fifth week the most competent students with Type III profiles had overlapped into the lower range of distribution of Type I students. (Distribution of the three students with Type IV profiles is obscured in Week one.)

In Examination: 1977 Cohort

The approximate distribution range of profile types was also mapped (Fig.

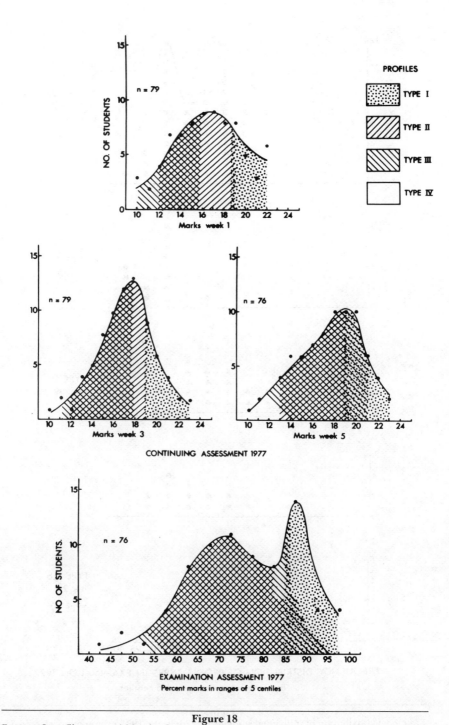

Figure 18
Range of profile types within the frequency distributions of scores from weekly tests and final examination in the 1977 cohort. Actual marks gained in 24 test items, for modules/weeks 1, 3 and 5; examination marks (scored out of 100 and therefore percentage scores); curves drawn as lines of closest fit.

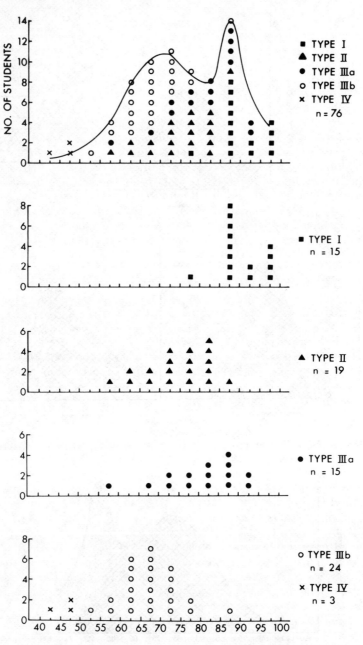

Figure 19
Frequency distribution of individual students (n=76) in the 1977 examination, classified as
profile types. The squares, triangles, circles and crosses summarize the types of students in
each range of 5 marks, separately as profile types, and together as the whole cohort, within
the skewed bimodal frequency distribution curve as in Fig. 9.

18) within the bimodal frequency distribution of the 1977 examination scores (see Fig. 9). It is apparent that some Type III students were at mastery level – ie they had maintained the level of scores gained in the fifth week (Fig. 18); some Type II students also achieved mastery, and therefore surpassed previous performance levels, while Type I students again demonstrated their superior capabilities and were confined almost entirely to the second peak of the bimodal curve.

Figure 19 shows the actual frequency distribution (in ranges of 5) of the examination scores of the seventy-six students in the 1977 cohort, classified by profile types. Of the thirty students who achieved mastery (80%) in examination, there were fourteen Type I (n=15); nine Type IIIA (n=15); six Type II (n=19); one Type IIIB (n=24). It was then evident that the Type III students who gained mastery (Fig. 18) were almost exclusively in the profile sub-type IIIA. So that whereas Type IIIA students carried improvement in performance across weekly tests over into examination, Type IIIB could not sustain their performance levels when tested by complex problems in examination.

PARAMETERS OF PROFILE TYPES
It is assumed that each student entered the course with a different level of ability or prior knowledge; developed at a different rate; attained different levels of performance and responded uniquely to the techniques of teaching used. Consequently, in the classification of the four major profiles types and two sub-types, emphasis was placed on: (i) *intercepts*, in all categories; (ii) *slope*, in all categories; (iii) *predicted outcome* (this chapter, Note 32), in final examination, based on performance in weekly tests; and (iv) the *actual examination score*.

Profile Types I - IV
Only four individual linear regressions are shown in the profile graphs; for clarity the summation of skills is shown only in Figures 16 and 17. A comparison of the predicted outcome and the actual examination score (shown in Figs. 20-22) lends credence to the demarcation between Profile Types I and II, and sub-Types IIIA and IIIB. The examination score on the profile graphs may be used to locate the position of each student – as a profile type – on the frequency distribution graph in Figure 19. As only one example of each profile type is illustrated in the graphs (Figs. 20-22), the outstanding characteristics (and variations) of the types are summarized in the text below and in Note 36 in this chapter. Performance outcomes are clearly represented in Figure 19, except for Type IV (example from 1975 cohort).

Types I and II show clearly distinct profiles based upon the parameters of intercept and examination outcome (Fig. 20), with both types showing little or no change in overall performance levels, as judged by the 'combined skills' profile (Fig. 16). For most Type I students, high entry levels apparently excluded any overall change, but this could be explained by the fact that most of the test items were not very discriminative for the best students, including all those in Type I. To remove this constriction effect in the upper range of the test scores would have required the introduction of more discriminating items – too demanding for the majority of students. With the

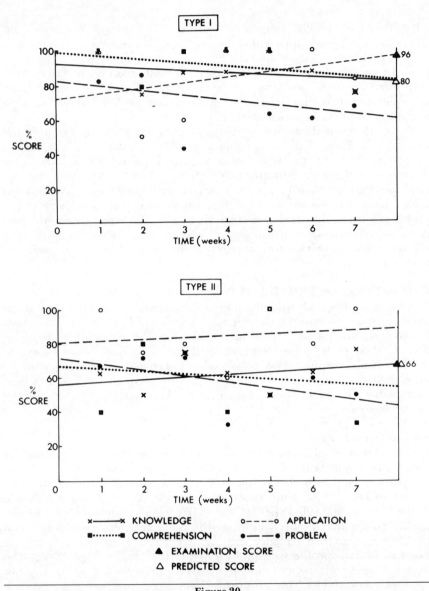

Figure 20

Characteristics of Profile Types I and II as regressions of performance with time in four cognitive categories, showing predicted and actual examination scores. Type I profile: top of the range; Type II: lower end (see Fig. 19).

tests administered, more than 20 per cent but less than 80 per cent of students responded correctly to nearly all individual test items. Nonetheless, since scores in final examination have usually exceeded outcomes predicted by the profiles for Type I students (Fig. 20) it is assumed that the learning experiences gained from this course also have benefited these students. This assumption was confirmed by their own evaluation of the course, and especially of group discussions (Chapter 8).

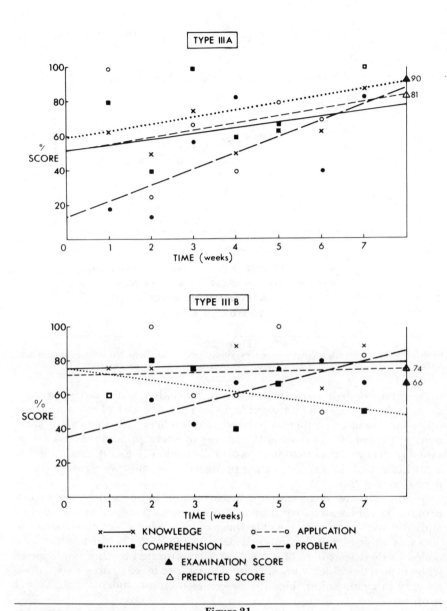

Figure 21
Characteristics of Profile Types IIIA and IIIB as regressions of performance with time in four cognitive categories, showing predicted and actual examination scores. Type IIIA profile: top of range; Type IIIB: lower end (see Fig. 19).

Learning profiles classified as *Type I* included the most successful students, judged by their overall performance in this subject at mastery (distinction) level (Fig. 19 and Table 17), and from achievement in other university courses (Table 20).

Students with *Type II profiles* could be described as average to fair students, with profiles significantly lower in cognitive parameters than in Type I. Although they did not improve significantly across weekly tests (Fig. 16),

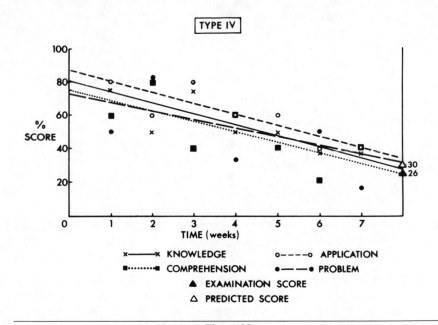

Figure 22
Characteristics of Profile Type IV as regressions of performance with time in four cognitive categories, showing predicted and actual examination scores (example from 1975 cohort).

they sustained their performance levels, but either could rarely improve their grades or were not motivated to do so. For some, lack of motivation was related to the fact that they were bonded as teachers (personal communication). Examination scores varied according to intercepts and covered a wide range of grades, from marginal pass to distinction (Fig. 19), and although some individuals far exceeded their predicted score most were close to those predicted (Fig. 20).

As the weekly tests contained assessment items which were both progressive and summative (building on previous knowledge of concepts and principles) it is also possible that students who maintained perform-ances, as judged by their combined skills profile (Fig. 17), must in fact have added to their learning. This has been demonstrated by those individuals with Type II profiles who surpassed their predicted scores and gained mastery in examination (Fig. 19) as well as by most students with Type I profiles.

It is apparent that the 'mediocre' students with *Profile Types IIIA,B* (Fig. 17) differ in prior experience and entry skills from those with Profile Types I and II. In weekly test performance, this type was characterized by a consistent increase in scores (steep regression slopes for IIIA,) effectively carried over to final examination in most Type IIIA profiles but less evident in final outcome for Type IIIB (Fig. 19). Significantly those Type III students with low intercepts in 'skills' categories do not deteriorate in weekly tests, although final outcomes (especially with Type IIIB) may often fall below those predicted (Fig. 21).

Examination scores allow differentiation between the two main sub-Types of Type III (Fig. 19), but slopes in the categories of problem solving and comprehension were the criteria used for this distinction (Fig. 21). As might be expected in Type IIIA, characterized by an increase in slopes for both problems and comprehension, predicted outcomes are usually matched and occasionally surpassed by actual examination scores (Fig. 21). For profiles similar to the sub-Type IIIB in Figure 21, the increase in slope for problems is apparently negated by a decrease in slope for comprehension, ie understanding of the course material (this chapter, Note 37). As the intercept for problems is also low (Note 37), predicted scores (for examination) were rarely attained and, not unexpectedly, are much lower than for Type IIIA. In another variation of the sub-Type IIIB, although there is little change in slope for problems, the intercept is higher than for many Type III profiles, and slopes for comprehension increase. Not unexpectedly, examination scores are better than in the sub-Type IIIB shown in Figure 21, but may fall below those predicted, and on average are not equivalent to those for Type IIIA.

In the frequency distribution of examination scores for profiles types in 1977 (Fig. 19), the majority of IIIB profiles similar to those in Figure 21 (9 out of 24) are in the lower part of the frequency range (< 65 per cent), but at least one of the other fifteen students with IIIB profiles (shown in Fig. 19) surpassed his predicted score and attained mastery. (The Type IIIA student who scored between 55-60 registered high examination anxiety.)

Type III students (particularly Type IIIA) showed the greatest response to the SIMIG method and presumably derived most benefit. The overall effectiveness of groups and the feedback from discussion and initial marking of test items have been reported by these students as the main reason for their improvement.

Type IV students (comprising less than 5 per cent of the entire sample) showed a general downward trend across the cognitive categories, but as intercepts were relatively high (Fig. 22), lack of ability may not have been the principal factor in determining this response. The consistent deterioration in performance indicates an increasing inability to integrate material from preceding modules, probably because of inadequate time spent in the learning centre (Table 18), associated with low interest and motivation. Subsequently, these students have either discontinued or repeated the year; most were disenchanted with university life, rather than with this course or teaching method (personal communication).

Variation in Frequency Distributions of Profile Types: 1975 - 1978
The distribution of students in profile types across years (Table 16) reflects the different abilities of the pairs of cohorts 1975/77 and 1976/78. Types I

Types	1975	1976	1977	1978
	n=106	n=71	n=76	n=59
I	20	16	20	17
II	33	39	25	47
IIIA	21	10	20	11
IIIB	22	29	31	20
IV	4	6	4	5

Table 16
Percentages of students in profile types from 1975 to 1978.

and IIIA, with the best outcomes (as judged by final examination), comprised 41 per cent and 40 per cent in 1975/77, compared with 26 per cent and 28 per cent in 1976/78. The relative proportions of students classified as Type IIIA to Type II showed the same trend, with higher proportions of Type IIIA profiles in 1975/77.

Profile Types and Mastery in Final Examination: 1975 - 1978

Performance at mastery level for students classified in profile types has been analysed for overall examination scores and for examination problems (Table 17). Over the four years of investigation (1975 - 1978) there was an increase in difficulty of problems and in the percentage of marks awarded to problems in examination; nonetheless, performance in examination problems increased significantly (Tables 7,8). It is therefore interesting that in each of the four years the only profile parameter which showed significant change (P<0.01) was that of problem-solving.

Profile Types	Percentage of Students in Profile Types with Mastery							
	1975		1976		1977		1978	
	n=106		n=71		n=76		n=59	
1 Mastery in Examination								
I	(21)	57	(11)	64	(15)	94	(10)	80
II	(35)	0	(28)	7	(19)	31	(28)	25
III	(46)	37	(28)	21	(39)	26	(18)	27
IV	(4)	0	(4)	0	(3)	0	(3)	0
2 Mastery in Examination Problems								
*	69%		76%		76%		80%	
I		48		73		94		80
II		0		0		31		17
III		17		11		39		27
IV		0		0		0		0

*Percentage marks contributed by problems to examination.

Table 17
Proportions of profile types gaining mastery in examination 1975-78. Percentage of students with mastery (80%) in: 1) total examination; and 2) problem questions in examination. Total number of students (in brackets) in the types shown for each year.

Within any year, the percentages of students in different profile types gaining mastery in overall examination, or in examination problems (Table 17), show that a majority of Type I students have gained mastery, while only some students from Types II and III achieved this level of performance. It should come as no surprise that Type IV students never attain mastery! Significantly more individual problem questions have been answered at mastery level by Type I students than by all other types in each year, while Type III (more specifically, IIIA) students have achieved mastery on more problem questions than Type II students.

In analysing performance between years (Table 17) consideration should be given to the average ability of the cohorts, to changes made in content of examination (Chapter 4), and to changes made to group discussions which had an impact on teaching and learning strategies.

Significantly more Type I students gained mastery in overall examination in 1977 (94 per cent, Table 17) than in 1975 (57 per cent, $z = 2.56$, P<0.01), and also in problem-solving questions ($z = 2.37$, P<0.01). Results for Type I students in 1976 and 1978 also reflect overall improvement with time, with performance in the 1978 cohort again surpassing that of all other years with the exception − not unexpected − of 1977.

It is in Types II and III that the effect of improvements in teaching strategies on problem-solving become most apparent. Whereas no student in Type II gained mastery in 1975, 31 per cent attained this level in 1977 both for overall examination and in problem-solving. In 1976, 7 per cent of Type II students reached mastery level in overall examination (by gaining mastery in some but not all problems). In 1978 outcomes for Type II were significantly better than in 1976 (for both overall mastery and mastery in problems), but not surprisingly somewhat below those for 1977 (Table 17). Similar improvements of performance in problem-solving are shown for Type III. Although results in 1977 for Type III students with mastery in overall examination (26 per cent) and mastery in problem solving questions (39 per cent) are somewhat anomalous, similar trends have already been noted in Chapter 4 for the whole cohort viz. 40 per cent (Fig. 4) and 46 per cent (Fig. 11) respectively.

OTHER STUDENT CHARACTERISTICS
Apart from the different cognitive characteristics of the profile types, as presented above, further validation of the typology is obtained from a consideration of other variables which might be expected to affect learning. Some of these attributes were routinely recorded for all students, eg interest in biology, general ability, age, sex, anxiety and time spent in module study. Where diversity appears between profile types, they are discussed below.

Interest in Biology
An estimate of the degree of interest in the subject was derived from items in a questionnaire given before the course began. These assessed enrolment preferences for biology, number of courses taken (current and contemplated for subsequent years), also rating of expectation of interest in the anatomy course and overall interest in biology II. Whereas Type II students were, on the whole, indifferent, the highest interest ratings were from Type III rather than Type I students, while the lowest interest was exhibited by Type IV students.

Age
Ages varied from eighteen to thirty years during the period 1975-78. As observed in previous years, older students, including those with mature age status, generally performed better than younger students; this may be related to their motivation to succeed. (The correlation of age with examination performance is statistically significant and has varied between 0.3 and 0.5.) It is difficult to correlate age with profile type: although not surprisingly these older students usually conformed to the patterns of Types I and IIIA. However, some of the youngest students with outstanding ability were also Type I. Most Type II students were young.

Time spent in Independent Study of Modules
Table 18 shows that there were some differences between profile types, and

between years, in the average time spent by students in the learning centre. Students in Type I and IIIA (ie most of those with mastery in examination) generally averaged more time in module study than all other types. The Type IV samples — always very small — scored the lowest overall mean.

Cohorts/ Years	I	Time Spent by Profile Types II	IIIA	IIIB	IV
1975	5.4	4.9	5.3	5.0	4.5
1976	5.9	5.4	6.2	5.2	5.5
1977	6.2	5.3	4.7	5.3	3.1
1978	5.1	4.8	5.7	4.5	5.0
Mean	5.7	5.1	5.3	5.2	4.6

Table 18
Mean time (hours) spent in independent study of modules by cohorts, classified as profile types, from 1975-78. Standard deviations are given in Note 38 in this chapter.

Table 18 gives no indication of the differences between individuals within each profile type. Type I students either spent an inordinately long time on the modules — using optional material — or effectively finished the modules in a short time. Type II students were erratic, some spending insufficient time, others appearing to spend time inefficiently. From responses to questionnaires in 1977 neither Type I nor Type II students spent much time in revision of modules before groups; this might be interpreted as indicating that, whereas Type I students did not require revision, Type II students were not sufficiently motivated to spend time in revision. Some Type III students averaged up to two hours in revision of modules prior to groups; Type IV students occasionally attempted revision before groups.

Anxiety
Two forms of the STAI test (see Appendix A: Records and Tests) were administered to provide measures of general anxiety (*Trait*) compared with that induced by final examination (*State*). The State test was administered in the examination room immediately prior to the commencement of the final examination, whereas the Trait test was given in the sixth group meeting. Many of the Type I students showed apparent 'exam stress' (that is, there was a considerable difference between normalized scores from the two forms of the test). One might surmise that this added pressure during examination 'fueled' their performance, but was not debilitating. Relatively high scores for general anxiety in Type I students also support the notion that some stress is required for optimal performance; even these students indicated that weekly test items frequently 'stretched' them. There was no significant difference between average scores for general anxiety in Types II and IIIB which were relatively low; but Type IIIA often had relatively high general anxiety. Types II and IIIA registered little or no exam stress, whereas many Type IIIB students (with low general anxiety) may have been adversely affected in examination by their relatively high exam stress. To summarize, Types I and IIIA registered highest general anxiety, and Types I and IIIB highest exam stress.

The tests in fact revealed few very high scores and this observation combined with personal responses from students in the questionnaires reported in the next chapter suggest that the SIMIG approach diminishes general anxiety or stress.

Sex Ratios

The sex ratios in profile types from the 1975-1978 cohorts (Table 19) show that the overall ratio for the sample (n=312) of males 3 : females 2 was maintained only in Profile Types I and IV. The lower ratio of females in Type II, and the higher ratios in Types IIIA and IIIB, may be interpreted as indicating that females were consistent in taking advantage of the teaching techniques — especially information exchange and discussion in groups — to improve their performance levels. In the above context, it is noteworthy that although the sex ratio for Type IIIB in 1977 (n = 24) was the same (1:1) as for the overall sample, ratios at the lower end of the frequency distribution were quite different. In Figure 19, all three students scoring <60% with Type IIIB profiles were males, as were seven of the nine Type IIIB students scoring <65%. However, the only Type IIIA student scoring <60% was a female with high exam stress.

	Profile Types					
	I	II	IIIA	IIIB	IV	Totals
Males	35	75	35	34	9	188
Females	23	34	28	33	6	124
Male:Female ratios	3:2	2:1	5:4	1:1	3:2	3:2

Table 19
Sex ratios in profile types from the 1975-78 cohorts.

Learning Preferences

Banks's Learning Styles Test (see Appendix A: Records and Tests) which estimates two continua of style — structured or unstructured and concrete or abstract — was routinely administered in the first and seventh week of the course. Specific learning preferences on the continua (evaluated from scores on twenty-two items) indicate whether an individual student prefers his material presented in a structured or unstructured way and whether it is coded in abstract (symbolic) or concrete terms. Generally, Type I students preferred less structured presentation than Type II students; Type III were more variable in their preferences. Significant changes (P<0.01) in the learning preferences of students towards structured and concrete (v. unstructured and symbolic) teaching occurred with this method of instruction, but there were no significant differences in changes of learning preferences between profile types.

General Ability

Table 20 provides data for comparison of previous academic performance with that in the SIMIG course for Profile Types I, II, IIIA and IIIB, in the 1977 cohort.

Measures of general ability (Table 20, items 1, 2, 3) were determined from previous attainment levels in:

1 The aggregate mark in Higher School Certificate, which determines entry to university.

2 The mean score for the preceding year: usually four first-year subjects in science, eg chemistry, physics, mathematics and biology.

3 The mean score for biology I, a prerequisite for biology II.

These results show that (for items 1, 2, 3) Type I students attained significantly higher scores (P<0.01) compared with other profile types. There were no significant differences between other types.

Performance As Mean Scores	Profile Types 1977			
	I	II	IIIA	IIIB
Previous	n=15	n=19	n=15	n=24
1 HSC (aggregate)	624	571	555	561
2 Preceding year	62.6	57.0	57.4	57.6
3 Biology I (pre-requisite)	72.0	58.8	60.3	62.2
SIMIG 1977				
4 Weekly tests	79.1 ± 2.3	71.5 ± 2.4	70.2 ± 2.9	68.5 ± 3.2
5 Final Exam	81.5 ± 1.4	66.3 ± 1.7	71.0 ± 2.3	63.0 ± 2.6

Table 20
Comparison of previous attainment levels with SIMIG scores for the profile types in the 1977 cohort. Previous academic performance (1, 2, 3) and performance in SIMIG (4, 5) shown as mean scores: aggregate mark for Higher School Certificate (HSC), percentages for items 2-5 (± standard deviation in 4, 5).

For both types of assessment in SIMIG (Table 20, items 4, 5), Type I students gained significantly higher scores (P<0.01), with means at or approximating mastery level, and from 8 to 18 per cent higher than for any other type. Between other types, there were no significant differences in means for weekly tests; but, not unexpectedly, examinations means for Type IIIA were significantly higher (P<0.05).

The mean score in biology I (Table 20, item 3) is therefore not a good predictor of performance in SIMIG, except for Type I students, most of whom perform well irrespective of the method of teaching and testing. The trend of improvement in average scores for biology I across Types II and IIIA and IIIB is reversed in continuing assessment scores for SIMIG (Table 20, item 4) although statistically not significant in both. As already noted, final examination scores (Table 20, item 5) for Type IIIA are significantly higher. In SIMIG, weekly tests and final examination are considerably more demanding than in biology I; nonetheless means in both SIMIG tests (Table 20, items 4, 5) are about 10 per cent higher in all types except Type IIIB. Although Type IIIB students improve during the SIMIG course in the weekly tests, most of them cannot respond to the challenge of the novel problems presented in final examination (see Fig. 19). It is not surprising therefore that their average examination marks are almost identical to those scored in biology I (Table 20, items 3, 5).

Deep or Surface Processing of Material Studied
A few days after the final examination in 1977, the most competent students were asked individually to recall their strategies for working through long-chain problems. The introspective accounts given indicated that those whose results comprised the 'second peak' in the bimodal distribution of scores in Figure 19 appeared to have employed the 'deep processing' of material described by Marton and Säljö (1976a). With 'surface processing',

there is a tendency to concentrate on memorizing facts or ideas.

Perusal of the examination scripts indicated that some students in the 'first peak' had also used a 'deep approach', but less successfully in that fewer problems were solved at mastery level. Students had been warned that the aims of the teaching would be matched by both assessment techniques: it appears that, in general, they had adopted (according to their individual ability) an approach 'determined by their expectations of what was required of them' (Marton and Säljö 1976b).

CONCLUSIONS

To classify students into categories of capacity to learn is, of course, a gross over-simplification of the complex outcome of nature and nurture which determines their behaviour. Yet, in the search for generalizations (essential in the methodology of science) it is worthwhile to make cautious classifications, as have been done for learning profiles. Bearing in mind, therefore, that information is lost when individuals are assigned to types, that the samples are small, and that the study refers only to one particular style of instruction in one course, nevertheless some tentative conclusions can be drawn or inferred from an examination of profile types.

In the classification of profile types presented here, the primary criterion used for the initial differentiation (Figs. 16 and 17) was relative change in performance in all the 'skills' in which measurement had been made (viz. comprehension, application and problem-solving). As all these skills require basic knowledge, it may have been expected that the profile in the category of 'recall of knowledge' would be an important indicator of student learning. This was not so, and indeed this profile showed more variation than those of all other skills. This lack of correlation with 'recall of knowledge' is important, and may be used as an argument for allowing textbooks to be used in examination − a feature of SIMIG exams. (A lot of good scientists have poor 'recall' − Charles Darwin emphasizes this in his autobiography − he himself had a poor capacity for recall.) Supporting evidence was obtained from results of multiple regression analyses. These showed that apart from the *intercept* for 'recall of knowledge', parameters relating to performance in this category were of little predictive significance to outcome performance in examination, and showed little relationship to performance in any of the 'skills' categories in weekly tests.

As the 1975-78 examinations had a high proportion (69 to 80 per cent) of complex problem-solving questions, it may have been expected that profiles for problem-solving would best predict examination outcomes, especially as they were the only parameters which showed significant change. However, the parameters of the 'combined skills' category (ie comprehension, application and simple problem-solving) were the *most accurate predictors of examination outcome*, better than the weighted predictor score which includes recall of knowledge, and significantly better than any of the individual parameters.

Although no practice was provided in groups for solving complex problems, students gained experience in the component skills required for the solution of these examination problems. From 1975, group sessions as a whole and weekly test items in particular were more sharply focused on exercising the separate skills used in problem-solving. If this strategy is effective, the performance of individuals in final examination should either be predictable, as in Type IIIA where students have 'learned' during the course and been able to maintain this performance in examination, or it should show an increase over and above performance in weekly tests, as in Type I. Support for this assertion has been provided from an analysis of mastery in overall performance in problem questions and in individual problem questions between the years 1972 - 1978 (Chapter 4).

For all types of profiles, comparisons of performance in examination provide additional information on the effects of changes in teaching strategies. Considering mastery in overall examination performance or in problem-solving (Table 17) Types I - III (inclusive) showed significantly improved outcomes between years. Differential student response to changes in teaching strategies may explain the evolution from negatively skewed (1969 - 1976) to skewed and bimodal (1977 and 1978) frequency distribution curves (Figs. 9 and 19) of performance in examination. It is interesting to see that, again, in 1978, performance of profile types at mastery level in overall examination and in problems was above that observed for profile types in previous years, with the exception of 1977 (Table 17).

One variable which might affect student learning and thus profile type is the difference in skills of the tutors in the groups. For example, in 1978 groups were taken by two members of staff with widely differing experience in group management. Although groups were 'matched' as far as possible on the basis of several criteria (prior achievement, sex ratios, interest, etc.), distribution of students from both tutors' groups into Profile Types II and III was significantly different within each type (x^2 = 42.80 and 20.25, P<0.05). The higher proportion in Type III and the lower proportion in Type II were from groups taken by the more experienced tutor (IMB). So some individuals with Type III profiles, who show significant improvement with time, may be responding to the skills of the tutor as well as to the teaching method.

NOTES 30 - 38

30　Linear regressions of performance with time: straight line of best fit (obtained statistically) from points representing test scores gained in each of the four categories, over seven weeks.

31　Only six sets of test scores were strictly comparable for the time : performance analysis (Chapter 6), but seven sets of scores in these categories were available for the graphs (in the eighth week the continuing assessment score was for a written report on the project) (see Appendix A: Records and Tests).

32　*Definitions of profile parameters*
　　Intercepts (entry behaviour) are derived by extrapolating regression lines to the ordinate axis for each of the cognitive categories of recall of knowledge, comprehension, application, and problem-solving, and also for a combined 'skills' category.
　　Slopes (rate of change in performance) are the lines obtained from linear regressions of performance in the different cognitive categories with time. With slopes, particular attention was directed to the summation of

the three 'skill' categories of comprehension, application and problem-solving, and individually particularly to the latter category, as indicators of rate of change of behaviour, ie learning.

Predicted outcome for examination is that predicted from the weighted predictor score over all four categories, by extrapolation.

33 *Criteria of change used in profile analysis*
Relative levels were used as criteria for change in slope (learning) based upon the numbers of questions in the different cognitive categories, so as to represent, in each case, a change in weekly test score (over the seven weeks) equivalent to one question in the category with the largest number of items − eight (prior to 1978) − in recall of knowledge. This represents a change in performance of approximately 2 per cent per week in each of the categories, which is approximately equivalent to a significant change ($P<0.05$) using a monotonic trend analysis.

Performance in any category can therefore be distinguished as showing either increase or decrease (greater than criterion level), or no change (less than criterion level). However, downward trends (also less than criterion levels), observed with students who have high intercepts in one or more of the cognitive categories, may result from the measurement techniques employed.

34 *Difficulty of weekly test items*
From 1976, the seven weekly tests were criterion referenced (as measured by student performance in previous years with sample size n∼300). There was no difference in difficulty of items within any category between years.

The Kuder Richardson$_{20}$ (KR_{20}) formula for a coefficient of reliability was used, as test items were marked either right or wrong.

The mean reliability coefficient for each module test over the period of the study was consistently high ($KR_{20} = 0.70 \pm 0.06$), considering the relatively small number of items per week. It is assumed, therefore, that these tests accurately monitor changes in performance both within and between years.

For each of the four categories, mean reliability coefficients were also high, notwithstanding the smaller number of items. The coefficients were: Recall of knowledge, 0.61 ± 0.10; Comprehension, 0.80 ± 0.80; Application, 0.63 ± 0.09; Problems, 0.71 ± 0.09. Thus reliability estimates on these four component classes were comparable with those calculated for the total twenty-four (1976-77) or sixteen items (1978) for each weekly test.

35 *The number of items* scored in each of the seven tests has been constant within each year: twenty-four items in 1976/77, with a reduction to sixteen in 1978. But an increase in cognitive demand of questions over years, expressed as a percentage of the constituents, was obtained by increasing the proportion of problems and decreasing the proportion of recall of knowledge items, from eight recall in 1976/77 to four in 1978 (together with three questions each in comprehension and application and six problems). The rationale for this was twofold: first it was thought

desirable to increase the number of open discussion questions, and second, the category of 'recall of knowledge' by itself had little predictive significance for final performance in examination.

36   *Characteristics of Profile Types*
Type I High intercepts (~80 − 100) in all categories; little change in performance with time in the combined skills profile (see Fig. 16).
    Across weeks performance in individual categories remained steady, or showed slight increases or decreases, but rarely changed significantly. Examination scores (usually more than 85%) exceed predicted scores.
Type II Lower intercepts (~50 − 80) than for Type I; little change in performance with time in the combined skills profile (see Fig. 16), counterbalancing variations in performance in individual categories. That is, across weeks, overall performance was sustained but rarely improved. Examination scores, usually similar to those predicted, ranged from marginal pass (50-59%) to credit and distinction (80-100%) (see Fig. 19), but were significantly lower than in Type I.
Type IIIA Marked improvement with time in the combined skills category (see Fig. 17, derived from the student profile in Fig. 21), due mainly to the steep regression slopes for problem-solving from very low intercepts (~20). Comprehension scores also improved from low intercepts (50-60); performance in application items varied according to intercepts. Examination scores similar to those predicted at credit to distinction level.
Type IIIB Improvement with time, as with all Type III profiles, in the combined skills category (see Fig. 17, derived from the student profile in Fig. 21). Two forms of Type IIIB are readily distinguishable; only one is represented by the example in Figure 21. Although intercepts for cognitive categories were variable, the slopes in problem-solving and comprehension were the criteria for this distinction. In Figure 21 the steep increase in the slope for problem solving (similar to Type IIIA) indicated a marked improvement with time, absent in the other form which had a higher intercept for problems. Similarly, whereas performance in comprehension decreased across weeks for the student shown in Figure 21, the other form of IIIB profile showed a marked increase in this skill.
    Examination scores were much lower than in Type IIIA, from marginal pass to credit (one distinction in 1977; see Figure 19).
Type IV Parameters cannot be defined concisely for such a small sample (5 per cent), but performance in all cognitive categories deteriorated with time. Intercepts were variable, often higher (Fig. 17) than in many Type III profiles. However, the downward pitch of these regression slopes, when extrapolated back to the ordinate axis, tends to exaggerate and therefore misrepresent the entry levels. As predicted, all Type IV students failed in final examination (Fig. 19).

37   *Factors which may explain the examination results of individuals with learning profiles classified as Type IIIB*
    i   From multiple regression analysis, using profile parameters as predictors of examination performance in 1977, it was found that total test scores both in problems, and in combined skills (ie

comprehension, application and problems) predicted total examination score (both at P<0.05).

ii From multiple regression analysis, using profile parameters as predictors of performance in weekly tests in 1977, total score for problems was predicted by intercept for problems (P<0.001) and total score in comprehension (P<0.01). This suggests that comprehension is an essential skill in problem-solving, and that although skills necessary for short-chain problem-solving may be learnt, increase in slope in (short-chain) problems in weekly tests (as with profile IIIB in Fig. 21) does not necessarily predict overall score in problem test items, nor in multiple-chain problem questions in final examination.

38 Standard deviations from Table 18 for time spent in module study:

Cohorts/ Years	I	II	Profile Types IIIA	IIIB	IV
1975	±0.30	±0.18	±0.29	±0.15	±0.49
1976	±0.53	±0.20	±0.28	±0.29	±0.62
1977	±0.25	±0.38	±0.18	±0.24	±0.59
1978	±0.48	±0.18	±0.37	±0.60	±1.10
Mean	±0.31	±0.22	±0.26	±0.28	±2.45

8 Evaluation of SIMIG

INTRODUCTION

The preceding chapters have recorded the detailed monitoring of student achievements during the experimental period 1969-78, with the statistical evidence. However, as Parlett and Hamilton argued in their seminal paper on 'illuminative evaluation' (1972), statistics of this kind say nothing of the personal responses of the staff or the students involved during the decade. With the object of maintaining a reasonably comprehensive picture of developments as they unfolded I also obtained, as Parlett and Hamilton suggest, evidence of a more subjective nature, from two sources. In the first place, during the whole period, approximately 1000 students (about 98 per cent of the total sample) have filled in questionnaires at the last group meeting, evaluating the whole course (Tables 21 - 23). In 1977, students obligingly used their enrolment number so that responses (previously anonymous) could be analysed in terms of profile types (Table 23). The same students completed – at a later date – a questionnaire comparing teaching methods and assessment procedures used in all courses in second-year botany in 1977 (Table 24).

Second, by talking to the students, and by actively canvassing and receiving feedback from demonstrators in the learning centre and in the groups, I gained a cumulative overview of the reactions of staff and students.

As tutor to four or five groups in each cohort for ten years, I became very conscious of the impact on the group of the physical environment in which it meets, and the importance of providing and maintaining a climate conducive to maximum interaction of group members. These impressions were useful in designing questionnaires to elicit overall student opinions.

OVERALL STUDENT RESPONSES

Student opinions of the SIMIG teaching method are presented in three sections: evaluations by cohorts of self-instructional modules (Table 21A) and of discussion groups (Table 21B, Table 22); and analysis of evaluations classified according to profile types (Table 23).

Evaluation of Self-instructional Modules

During the period 1969-71, before the distinctive, slide-based group work was introduced, the focus of attention in the questionnaires was on the self-instructional work. One item: 'Rate the effectiveness of audio-tutorial (A-T) self instruction as opposed to lecture/lab. classes in other science subjects', gained a 95 per cent positive (much more effective or more effective) rating in 1969 and rarely less than 90 per cent in subsequent years. Of five students who failed the course in 1968 (with traditional teaching) and repeated in 1969, all preferred A-T instruction.

Especially in the first three years, feedback from students' optional weekly comments (with a 'drop-in' suggestion box) were useful in the yearly revisions of each module, particularly of the audiotapes. The questions on these anonymous evaluation forms were typical open-ended inquiries such as:

'What were the best features of this week's module?'

'What were the worst features of this week's module?'

'Other comments.'

During this period, the overall reaction of students to self-instruction in carrels was also canvassed, with a view to responding, where possible, to reasonable complaints. Three questions asked were:

1 'List the worst features of self-instruction.'
2 'List the best features of self-instruction.'
3 'Any other comments?'

The following are examples of students' personal responses to these questions:

1 *List the worst features of self-instruction*

'Very strenuous − one really feels like a good rest after going through an audio-visual programme, especially in one sitting.'

'It is hard to concentrate on the tapes for long lengths of time.'

'Not enough space in the carrels to work comfortably.'

'The headphones give me a headache.'

'Listening to one voice is monotonous.'

2 *List the best features*

'I can work at my own pace.'

'Practical and theory combined increases interest in the subject.'

'With the self-quizzes in the study guide, and feedback from the audiotape, I can be sure as I go along that I understand the work properly and have covered it in as much depth as I want to.'

'I like being allowed to come into the learning centre at any time.'

'Open access to lab. means I can look at demonstrations or tape-slides when I have an hour free between lectures.'

'Detailed overall picture is obtained and relevant function of plant organs is fully explained as well as the anatomy and accompanied by full notes.'

'I am sure that I have learnt the work more thoroughly than if we had conventional-type practical work.'

3 *Other comments*

'The method of teaching has induced a liking for the subject − mainly because I'm learning and understanding more of it than in other subjects.'

'A most enjoyable and profitable course!'

'Found course up to date most interesting and I believe the carrel method has helped me learn much, and quickly.'

'Personal contact with other students is reduced but this is largely overcome by the group work.'

'Overall a good method of teaching, however groups are essential in combination to avoid complete loss of personal relations.'

'I have enjoyed the course. This department is much more flexible and helpful than most. The work is well and interestingly arranged; concern with students' preferences and problems is very gratifying.'

'I appreciate the emphasis on student participation.'

'In terms of time spent, learning efficiency is greatly increased with recall of material being much greater, even after 9 weeks without revision.'

The staff met the complaints (worst features) by:

a   Providing tea/coffee facilities at minimal cost in the learning centre.
b   Buying padded headphones.
c   Reorganizing the audiotapes so that listening periods did not exceed 5 minutes.
d   Limiting total length of audiotape to 45-50 minutes.
e   Alternating male/female voices in the audiotape.
f   Extending the desk space of each carrel.

The period 1974-76 is represented by Table 21. Table 21 A, items 1-5, refer to the overall SIMIG method and to self-instruction. Table 21 B, items 6-8, refer to groups.

Because of individual differences in learning preferences, one method of instruction will usually please some students but alienate others. From Table 21A reactions of the 1974/76 cohorts to the *SIMIG method* were positive (item 1) and similar figures for overall responses were obtained from question-naires in subsequent years. Students were satisfied with the integration of material in *carrel programmes* (item 2) and with *demonstrations* (item 3). Routine *demonstrating* of carrel material (item 4) was required only 'occasionally' to 'hardly ever'; this was interpreted as a favourable response to overall presentation and explanation of material by annotated photomicro-graphs and other media.

The ratings for content and interest in *tape-slides* (item 5) were positive for more than 80 per cent of each cohort over the whole period. Another aspect canvassed in 1977 confirmed that students regarded the anatomy tape-slides as fulfilling the objective of providing reinforcement of learning done in the carrels (92 per cent positive) and less as additional information (66 per cent). Students were advised to look at this tape-slide on completion of module study, and some members of the same groups (58 per cent) also met regularly in 1977 to review and discuss the relevant tape-slide immediately prior to the group sessions.

Table 21 shows the weight of positive responses from students, but the following extracts from questionnaires provide a more vivid picture of their personal responses to self-instruction during the period 1974 to 1976.

With the audio-visual method I have more time to digest the material. Live lectures confuse me and I cannot keep up with what is being said, as by the time I've finished writing one point I've missed the next.'

'A more comprehensive way of understanding subject matter.'

'Occasionally I resent the fact that I cannot pursue all the interesting material fully.'

'I find this method of practical work far more refreshing than in the traditional form. The tape-slide programmes expand carrel information

		Percentage Responses					% Positive Responses Categories
		1	2	3	4	5	(1 and 2)

A Questionnaire items on SIMIG method (1) and self-instruction (2 - 5)

		1	2	3	4	5	(1 and 2)
1 Rate your overall reaction to the *SIMIG*	1974	30	62	6	2	0	92
teaching-learning *methods* used in plant	1975	29	56	9	4	2	85
anatomy (very effective to very ineffective)	1976	48	48	1	3	0	96
2 Rate your reaction to the *carrel programmes*							
with reference to integration of theory/	1975	27	51	11	7	4	78
practical	1976	27	64	8	1	0	91
3 Rate your reaction to the *demonstrations*	1975	21	58	20	2	0	79
in the learning centre	1976	27	50	22	1	0	77
4 Have you relied on *demonstrator* help in	1974	0	6	54	34	6	6
interpreting material studies in the carrel?	1975	1	8	58	26	7	9
(very much, much, occasionally, hardly	1976	0	7	68	20	5	7
ever, never)							
5 Rate your reaction to the *tape-slides* in the							
learning centre with regard to content and	1975	25	55	18	1	1	80
interest	1976	46	46	7	1	0	92

B Questionnaire items on work in groups (6-8)

		1	2	3	4	5	(1 and 2)
6 Rate your reaction to *continuing assessment*							
(in small groups), by written answers to							
questions usually related to slide	1975	22	51	19	8	1	73
projections of plant material	1976	20	73	7	0	0	93
7 Rate your overall reaction to group	1974	30	53	15	1	1	83
sessions with regard to *content*	1975	15	68	16	1	1	83
	1976	13	80	7	0	0	93
8 Rate your reaction to the group *tutor* in							
terms of interest displayed in you as an							
individual (very interested and friendly,							
interested, indifferent, not interested, very	1975	19	56	19	6	0	75
disinterested and unfriendly)	1976	28	63	8	1	0	91

Table 21
Course evaluation questionnaires 1974-76. Responses in five categories from very positive (1) to very negative (5) expressed as percentages of each cohort. Percent positive responses (Categories 1 and 2) also shown. 1974 (n=114), 1975 (n=104), 1976 (n=70).

and provide interesting and additional points.'
'Better than lectures and labs because of the variety of activities.'
'The audiotape puts all relevant data and other information in perspective – very well organized – a good basis for further investigation. The tape-slide programmes are very helpful as well as interesting. I find it easier to concentrate when the relevant visual aid is accompanied by explanation.'
'I prefer lectures and lab work.'
'Self-instruction probably suits most people, but I find it is too impersonal and dull.'
'I don't like the teaching method much, although it is obvious that staff are enthusiastic, and this is appreciated by all students.'

'I did not particularly like audiotapes, but considering the type of factual information being taught, I found it much more effective than a conventional detailed approach as in invertebrate zoology, or rocks and minerals in geology.'

Evaluation of Group Work

To find out whether my aims for the group sessions were being achieved, the opinion of students was sought on all aspects of the groups.

Responses to items used in the 1974/76 cohorts are shown in Table 21B. Most students reacted favourably to the system of scoring tests in groups for *continuing assessment* (item 6) and the *content* of group sessions was regarded favourably (item 7). Not all cohorts were equally impressed with their group *tutor's attitude* (item 8): in 1976 90 per cent of the students thought their group tutor was friendly and personally interested in them as individuals; in 1975 only 75 per cent of them were so favourably impressed. In 1976, the

Questionnaire Items		Percentage Categories					% Positive Responses Categories (1 and 2)
		1	2	3	4	5	
1 Rate your overall reaction to the *SIMIG method* of teaching-learning (very	1977	42	57	1	0	0	99
effective to very ineffective)	1978	49	43	4	4	0	92
2 How effective is the small group session	1976	39	46	13	2	0	85
as a *learning experience* for you? (very	1977	31	59	9	1	0	90
effective to very ineffective)	1978	49	33	14	4	0	82
3 How much has *understanding of the module* (completed in SIM the previous week) improved after the group session?	1977	14	48	38	0	0	62
(very greatly to not at all)	1978	42	37	14	4	3	79
How much have groups aided you in the following categories? (Answer questions 4 to 9 using very greatly to not at all)							
4 *Recall* of basic facts and concepts	1977	6	50	39	5	0	56
	1978	16	57	13	11	3	73
5 Re-inforcement of *observation* of anatomical features by the use of slide	1977	24	68	8	0	0	92
transparencies (visual recall)	1978	40	45	15	0	0	85
6 *Comprehension*, ie understanding or interpreting anatomical features in	1977	13	69	18	0	0	82
projected slides	1978	41	46	11	2	0	87
7 *Application* of knowledge to previously	1977	8	41	49	2	0	49
unseen material, or in a different context	1978	27	48	25	0	0	75
8 *Analysis* of a problem question by	1977	9	33	50	7	1	42
interaction with peers or tutor	1978	32	41	24	3	0	73
9 *Evaluation*, ie selecting those items of greatest significance in a particular	1977	8	49	41	2	0	57
context and discarding others	1978	36	42	20	2	0	78

Table 22

Questionnaire Items		Percentage Categories					% Positive Responses Categories
		1	2	3	4	5	(1 and 2)
10 Regardless of the mark you achieve, do you feel *intellectually 'stretched'* by the test items? (Answer items 10-13 using (1) always, (2) often, (3) occasionally, (4) rarely and (5) never)	1977	21	37	34	8	0	58
	1978	34	37	22	5	2	71
11 Does *initial marking* of your own test papers contribute to the learning process?	1977	41	49	4	4	2	90
	1978	57	38	3	2	0	95
12 Does the *tutor facilitate* group interaction and discussion, eg encourage group members to find the answers to test items for themselves; ask another leading question where possible; contribute knowledge; or summarize only when the group requires some authoritative input?	1977	40	54	4	2	0	94
	1978	42	43	9	4	2	85
13 Is *continuing assessment* in groups psychologically *stressful* to you?	1976	5	17	47	14	17	22
	1977	6	17	27	36	14	23
	1978	13	27	27	24	9	40
14 Is the small group meeting an *enjoyable experience* for you? (very enjoyable, enjoyable, sometimes, not enjoyable, distressing)	1976	10	51	28	7	4	61
	1977	8	44	34	10	4	52*
	1978	21	40	27	10	2	61
15 Is your enjoyment of the group experience adversely affected by marking of test items for *continuing assessment*? (very much, much, occasionally, rarely, never)	1976	4	13	56	17	10	17
	1977	24	19	32	22	3	43
16 If written answers in group sessions were *not scored for assessment*, but used only for feedback on your performance, would you attend? (very positive to very negative)	1977	36	39	20	4	1	69
	1978	59	29	5	7	0	88
17 Approximately how much time (average/week) in hours, have you spent *revising anatomy* before group sessions (apart from the time spent on the module)?	hours	3	2	1½	1	¾ - ½	0
	1977	–	13	35	28	21	3
	1978	18	25	20	26	11	0
18 Approximately how much *time* (average/week) in hours, have you spent in the learning centre completing the module (carrel programme, tape-slides and demonstrations)?	hours	8	7	6	5	4	3
	1977	–	16	28	35	20	1
	1978	7	11	31	29	18	4

*Compare with 80% ('hindsight') in Table 24, Item 5.

Table 22
Course evaluation questions on aspects of group work 1976-78: responses in five categories from very positive (1) to very negative (5) expressed as percentages of each cohort; percentage of positive responses (1 and 2) also shown; 1976 (n=70), 1977 (n=76) and 1978 (n=64); some items on groups were used in 1976, others not until 1977. (*Table continued overleaf.*)

increase in the percentage of positive responses to these three items (6-8) may well reflect the improved 'climate' of the 1976 group sessions, when an increase from one to one and a half hours in the group sessions was made possible by a decrease in the numbers of students from 115 to 70.

Table 22 is essentially a report on how the 1977 and 1978 cohorts regarded the group work; where the same questions were first used in 1976, responses from this cohort are also shown.

Item 1 in Table 22 again confirms the favourable responses to the overall SIMIG method, and ratings for the group as an *effective learning experience* (item 2) were reassuringly high (80-90 per cent). In item 3, the lower percentage of positive responses is hardly surprising, as many students had already mastered most of the *content of the module* before group meetings.

Items 4 to 9 indicate how students perceived group activities as aiding them in various cognitive skills. Although between 80-90 per cent thought that group sessions helped them both in *visual recall* and *comprehension* (items 5 and 6), understandably a much lower percentage (especially in 1977) indicated that recall of basic facts and concepts (item 4) was aided by group work. As an aid to the skills of *application, analysis and evaluation* (items 7, 8, 9), responses were remarkably consistent within years, but between years consistently higher positive responses were recorded by the 1978 cohort. It is interesting, and perhaps an indication of the value of the SIMIG course for students of middling capacity, that it was the 1978 cohort that had the most mediocre average score in the school-leaving examinations (Table 2). The fact that approximately 50 per cent of the 1977 students perceived that discussion groups had only a marginal effect in aiding them in these skills (items 8, 9, 10), is also noteworthy. So, too, is the response from the small minority of students who showed aversion to discussion groups (categories 4 and 5). For most students, discussion groups undoubtedly helped them to learn.

Student reactions to other aspects of groups are summarized by responses to items 10 to 16 in Table 22. Even the best students admitted that some of the test items *stretched them intellectually* (item 10). Again positive responses to item 10 were higher in 1978. *Initial marking of test items in their own papers* (by a tick, cross or question mark) was regarded as a useful exercise by over 90 per cent of students (item 11). Most students also felt that the *tutor encouraged free discussion and interaction* (item 12) rather than dominated the group.

It is interesting to note that multiple regression analysis of student responses in 1977 to items in the course evaluation questionnaire showed that students' perception of:

1   The effectiveness of small groups predicted ($P<0.001$) their overall reaction to the SIMIG method.
2   The groups as an aid to skills of application and analysis also predicted ($P<0.05$) their overall reaction to SIMIG.
3   The groups as an aid to visual recall predicted ($P<0.05$) their understanding of the modules (ie feedback).
4   The students' enjoyment of groups predicted ($P<0.05$) their perception of the effectiveness of group sessions.

While many students really *enjoyed the group experience* (item 14), about 20 per cent in 1976/77, and about 40 per cent in 1978 admit to being *stressed* most of the time (item 13) and these percentages are confirmed by a similar question in item 15. However, 50 per cent of the students were rarely or *never stressed* in 1977, whereas in 1976/78 responses in these categories were reduced to about 30 per cent (item 13). These observed differences are consistent with the known differences between the abilities of the 1976/78 and 1977 cohorts. The interpretation of stress (personal communication from students) varied widely from a general state of anxiety before tests to a sense of being 'stretched' by particular test items: certainly the 1978 cohort registered higher stress levels (in the trait/state test on anxiety) than were recorded for the 1977 cohort.

It is well known that students easily find excuses to absent themselves from group discussions. By having tests, I introduced an element of compulsion. However, in hindsight, students affirmed that they would have attended the groups even if group tests had not been *scored for continuing assessment* (item 16); though I doubt whether they would have done so without having experienced SIMIG groups. Attendance in the groups was probably regulated by the percentage of marks given in relation to course assessment. In two subsequent courses/terms, with only 10% allocated, attendance was often irregular.

Responses to items 17 and 18 confirmed that the average *time spent in module study* was five and a half hours (see Table 13), while time spent outside the learning centre averaged one to one and a half hours. This is in contrast to what occurs in courses taught by conventional methods, where considerably more time is spent in private study.

Tables 21B and 22 show the weight of ratings given by students to particular aspects of group work, but the following examples reflect their personal responses to this method of learning in groups.

'Slides in the group discussions help to refresh memory and clarify doubtful points.'

'One learns a lot in the groups; being able to point to features on projected slides.'

'Makes me learn the work week by week, so I discover my problems instead of letting them accumulate. Also, having slides to look at, I learn by seeing, which makes it possible to really understand.'

'It is obvious that a lot of work goes into preparing these discussion questions (and tests) and into finding out our reactions – it is really very much appreciated.'

'The slides shown in groups and the discussions of these clarifies a great deal about the previous week's work, but I think more would be learnt if we were not doing tests at the same time.'

'I think weekly tests should be worth more – very useful to most students.'

'I think I might have got more out of the small group sessions (1½ hours) if there had been no written quizzes to do, thus allowing more genuine discussion. Anyhow, I thought the whole scheme was great.'

VARIATION OF RESPONSE AMONG PROFILE TYPES

In 1977 students were asked to use their course enrolment numbers on questionnaires (previously anonymous), so responses could be related to profile types. All students obliged, probably because they knew this was part of my research into the value of the techniques we were using. Table 23 presents the 1977 results broken down according to profile types.

In analysing the responses for profile types, the small sample size in each type (expressed as a percentage in the categories) should be taken into account; for this reason responses from Type IV (n = 3) have been omitted. Between profile types interesting differences in ratings for specific items were analysed and are summarized in Table 23.

Questionnaire Items	Profile Type	Percentage Categories					% Positive Responses Categories (1 and 2)
		1	2	3	4	5	
1 Rate your overall reaction to the *SIMIG method* of teaching-learning (very effective to very ineffective)	I	60	40				100
	II	45	55				100
	IIIA	43	57				100
	IIIB	21	75	4			96
2 How effective is the small group session as a *learning experience* for you?	I	27	60	13			87
	II	15	85				100
	IIIA	43	50	7			93
	IIIB	46	38	12	4		84
3 How much has *understanding of the module* (completed in SIM the previous week) improved after the group session? (very greatly to not at all)	I	7	40	53			47
	II	10	55	35			65
	IIIA	36	50	14			86
	IIIB	8	54	38			62
How much have groups aided you in the following categories? (very greatly to not at all)							
4 *Comprehension* ie understanding or interpreting anatomical features in projected slides	I	6	67	27			73
	II	20	70	10			90
	IIIA	19	60	21			79
	IIIB	4	79	17			83
5 *Application* of knowledge to previously unseen material, or in a different context	I		40	60			40
	II	10	25	65			35
	IIIA	14	36	43	7		50
	IIIB	12	38	50			50
6 *Analysis* of a problem question by interaction with peers or tutor	I	13	27	53	7		40
	II	5	25	65	5		30
	IIIA	21	36	29	7	7	57
	IIIB	4	50	38	8		54
7 *Evaluation*, ie selecting those items of greatest significance in a particular context and discarding others	I	6	27	47	20		33
	II	5	55	40			60
	IIIA	14	57	29			71
	IIIB	12	42	46			54
8 Regardless of the mark you achieve, do you feel *intellectually 'stretched'* by the *test items?*	I	20	47	33			67
	II	25	25	35	15		50
	IIIA	14	29	50	7		43
	IIIB	26	44	26	4		70
9 Does *continuing assessment* by test items in groups provide *incentive/motivation to learn?*	I	47	40	13			87
	II	30	45	20	5		75
	IIIA	22	57	14		7	79
	IIIB	42	42	12	4		84

Table 23

Questionnaire Items	Profile Type	Percentage Categories					% Positive Responses Categories (1 and 2)
		1	2	3	4	5	
10 Is *continuing assessment* in groups	I		13	40	27	20	13
psychologically *stressful* to you?	II	10	10	30	35	15	20
	IIIA		22	36	36	6	22
	IIIB	8	17	13	49	13	25
11 Is the small group meeting an *enjoyable*	I		47	40	13		47
experience for you? (very enjoyable,	II		50	40	10		50
enjoyable, sometimes, not enjoyable,	IIIA	14	50	22	14		64
distressing)	IIIB	9	35	39	4	13	44
12 Does *initial marking* of your own test	I	53	47				100
papers contribute to the learning	II	35	55	5		5	90
process?	IIIA	50	36		7	7	86
	IIIB	35	46	4	4		92
13 Does the *tutor facilitate* group interaction	I	47	53				100
and peer discussion?	II	20	80				100
	IIIA	50	50				100
	IIIB	50	33	13	4		83

Table 23
Evaluation of SIMIG group work by profile types: percentage responses by Profile Types I-III for the 1977 cohort to questionnaire items scored in five categories from (1) very positive to (5) very negative; % positive responses (categories 1 and 2) also shown; Type I (n=15), Type II (n=19), Type IIIA (n=15), Type IIIB (n=24).

Item 1: Analysis of responses has shown that the *SIMIG method* was rated favourably (categories 1 and 2) by all profile types. Moreover, a significant proportion of Type I students preferred the rating of 'very effective', whereas 'effective' (category 2) was equally popular with Types II and IIIA and preferred by Type IIIB. The higher ranking by Type I students is noteworthy, as it may be assumed that their performance would be less dependent on teaching method than students in other profile types.

Item 2 It is a reflection of their perceived improvement in weekly tests that groups were rated as 'highly effective' *learning experiences* for more students in Types IIIA and IIIB than for Types I and II, although there was little difference between types in the overall positive response.

Item 3 Students in Type IIIA were more positive than those in Types II and IIIB that their *understanding of module content* improved in the group meeting. In contrast, Type I responses to this item were split between 'improved' and 'marginally improved' (categories 2 and 3), for these students had mastered most of the module content before group meetings.

Items 4-7 (Gains in individual cognitive skills, eg comprehension, application, analysis and evaluation.) Analysis of items relating to specific gains in skills associated with *problem-solving* indicated that students in Type IIIA generally felt that they acquired more than those with Type II or IIIB profiles. This contrasts with responses to gains in *recall of knowledge* and *visual recall* (Table 22, items 4 and 5) where there was no difference between types (items not tabled). Students in Types II and IIIA placed particular emphasis on groups as aids to the development of skills of *comprehension and evaluation*, while at least 50 per cent of the students in Types IIIA and IIIB felt that groups improved their *analytical skill*. Not unexpectedly, the ratings for students with Type I profiles were lower; they were competent enough anyway to comprehend most of the material presented in groups. Nonetheless, most of them were not bored; they rated test items in groups as 'of sufficient difficulty to ensure interest'.

Item 8 Most Type IIIB students, as one might expect, felt that *test items* stretched them intellectually. Only about 25 per cent of them rated test items as 'too difficult', whereas responses from Types II and IIIA were equally divided between test items being 'intelligent and fair', and 'of sufficient difficulty to ensure interest'. Some Type I students were stretched by the test items too, and this is probably because they had wit enough to recognize that some of the items could be answered correctly in more than one way! However, very few ever gained full marks in any weekly test.

Item 9 Most students agreed that *continuing assessment* was a positive *motivating force in learning*; there was little difference in percentage positive responses between profile types.

Item 10 Approximately 20 per cent of Types II and III were always or often *stressed by* scoring of test items for *assessment*, while at least 50 per cent were rarely or never stressed (category 5) (thus corresponding to responses for 1977 in Table 22, item 13). The lowest anxiety ratings were in Type IIIB, although many of these students registered high exam stress.

Item 11 Students in Type IIIA gave the highest ratings to enjoyment of *group meetings*; responses for other types were split between categories 2 and 3. The positive responses for enjoyment in groups corresponds with responses from Type I and Type II students who perceived they were rarely or never stressed (45 per cent for Type I and 50 per cent for Type II). This suggests that while some individuals enjoyed the groups, for others — the anxious ones — enjoyment was marred by the need to score written responses for continuing assessment.

Item 12 In all profile types, at least 85 per cent rated feedback from *initial marking* and discussion of test items in groups as positive aids to learning. Type I students probably appreciated this type of feedback in groups more as confirmation, rather than new (operant) learning, as perhaps with Type III.

Item 13 All students thought that *tutors* helped to promote discussion in the groups, though there was some variation among types as to whether the tutor 'always' or 'usually' helped.

Although students with Type IV profiles (5 per cent of sample) usually rated the overall SIMIG method favourably, not unexpectedly their responses to the above items on groups were often either indifferent/ undecided or negative (categories 3, 4 and 5).

COMPARATIVE EVALUATION OF ALL BOTANY COURSES 1977

One possible explanation of this favourable response to SIMIG is, of course, that students like to 'please the teacher', and are unwilling to hurt the feelings of those who have obviously taken great trouble to make the course interesting. Naturally I had colleagues who were as concerned as I was to teach attractively and well, but who were doing so on conventional lines. So, to make sure that the results recorded in this chapter were not due merely to benevolence, I canvassed the opinions of the same students — at the end of

Questionnaire Items		Number* of Responses	\	Percentage of Categories				Response Summary		
			1	2	3	4	5	Mean Response	% Positive	% Negative
1 In terms of *difficulty*, compare your botany course(s) with other subjects taken this year (Categories 1-5 much more difficult to much less difficult)		(n=75)	5	6	73	16	0	0.0	11	16
2 Rate your *interest* (as a whole) in the botany course(s) taken (Categories 1-5 very interesting to dull)		(n=75)	23	60	11	5	1	1.32	83	6
3 Rate your reactions in terms of interest in *course content* to courses taken (short or full) (Categories 1-5 very interesting to dull)	Plant anatomy (a)	(n=75)	31	52	12	5	0	1.08	83	5
	Course b	(n=55)	42	36	15	5	2	1.13	78	7
	Course c	(n=55)	11	47	25	11	6	0.47	58	17
	Course d	(n=75)	27	40	13	13	7	0.70	67	20
4 Rate your overall reaction to group sessions as a *learning experience*, in each course taken (Categories 1-5 very favourable to very unfavourable)	Plant anatomy (a)		66	31	1	1	1	1.60	97	2
	Course c		11	40	24	12	13	0.20	51	25
	Course d		3	19	22	34	22	-0.40	22	56
5 Rate your overall reaction to *enjoyment* of group sessions (Categories 1-5 very enjoyable to very distressing)	Plant anatomy (a)		31	49	19	1	0	1.09	80	1
	Course c		13	27	36	18	6	0.20	40	24
	Course d		7	15	41	21	16	-0.10	22	37
6 Rate your overall reaction to *content* (relevant to course objectives) of group sessions (Categories 1-5 very favourable to very unfavourable)	Plant anatomy (d)		61	32	7	0	0	1.50	93	0
	Course c		18	33	33	11	5	0.50	51	16
	Course d		1	34	37	10	18	-0.10	35	28
7 Rate your reaction to the relevance and fairness of the methods of *assessment* used in courses (taken by you) (Categories (1) very fair, (2) reasonable, (3) adequate, (4) not relevant to perceived achievement, and (5) irrelevant and unfair)	Plant anatomy (d)		59	40	1	0	0	1.6	99	0
	Course b		38	35	20	7	0	1.0	73	7
	Course c		23	43	25	5	4	0.7	66	9
	Course d		0	19	37	29	15	-0.7	19	44

Table 24

*The number of responses (75 and 55) was consistent for each course; twenty students (ie 75-55) who were enrolled for the first half of the year were unavailable at the end of year as their course work had been completed.

Comparative evaluation of all courses in botany 1977. 'Questionnaire – October 1977 [Your answers to items in this questionnaire will provide us with information about your experience of different teaching methods in biology (botany strand) which may be useful in planning courses in later years. Answer only those items referring to courses taken by you]'.

In the response summary, the percentage positive responses (Categories 1 and 2) are balanced against the percentage negative responses (Categories 4 and 5). The rating for Category 3 is undecided, the same, indifferent, etc., according to the question. The mean response is calculated by giving a numerical value of $+2$, $+1$, 0, -1, -2 to each response in Categories 1 to 5, with the sum divided by the total number of responses. The maximum value is $+2$ and the minimum -2 (see text).

the year — about other courses in second-year botany in 1977.* The results
(Table 24) showed that this possible explanation would not account for the
favourable attitudes to SIMIG by cohorts from 1969-1978. They showed also
that students could on occasion be uncomfortably discriminating in their
evaluations.

Table 24 shows that:

i   There was no perceived difference in degree of difficulty between
    botany and other courses taken by the same students (mean response
    O, item 1).
ii In general, students found the various courses in second-year botany
    quite interesting (mean 1.32, item 2).
iii Course b and plant anatomy were rated much more highly in terms of
    interest in course content (mean 1.13 and 1.08, item 3).
iv The relevance and fairness of assessment methods were rated highest
    in anatomy (mean 1.6, item 7).
v   In items related to group sessions (scheduled as coursework) ratings
    were highest for plant anatomy in 'groups providing a learning
    experience' (mean 1.6, item 4), 'enjoyment of groups' (mean 1.09, item
    5), and 'content of group sessions with relevance to course objectives'
    (mean 1.5, item 6).

CONCLUSIONS: 1 STUDENT OPINION

Course evaluation questionnaires have mainly been used to gain an
impression of the effectiveness of the teaching, and, especially since 1974, of
the techniques used in the groups. Analysis of examination results is one way
of testing whether students measure up to the course supervisor's expectations, also to the aims and objectives of the course, but evaluations by
students are irreplaceable in that they provide the opinion of those on the
receiving end.

Students' perceptions of all aspects of teaching, the effectiveness of the
course in presentation, content, communication, opportunities for learning,
feedback, assessment and interest generated must be regarded as valid
estimates, given on completion of course work. All questionnaires were
prefaced by the phrase 'your opinions on the items in this questionnaire may
provide information for improving the course in the following year.'

Particularly with innovations in teaching, questionnaires also provide an
independent means of evaluation which may be useful in preserving one's
own sense of perspective, or as an insurance against colleagues critical of the
innovation.

Students were also very helpful in the comments they made directly to me,
particularly in the first years. They were very much aware that they could
contribute, even in a small way, to the success of this innovation, which in
itself was a novel experience in a university where all science-based subjects
followed the lecture-lab syndrome.

There can be little doubt that the popularity with which self-instruction
was received in 1969 had not diminished by 1978. Approximately 85-90 per
cent of each cohort from 1969 to 1978 were of the opinion that it was an

*This questionnaire was first circulated to other lecturers-in-charge of courses for their
comments, and permission for students to complete their responses in the final practical
class of the year.

effective method of learning, and more effective than other teaching methods employed for similar subjects. (However, it should not be inferred that they would have preferred all courses to be taught by a similar method.) There was of course a minority (about 5 per cent) who were not favourably impressed, and others who were indifferent. This is to be expected, as any method of teaching and learning cannot be equally effective for all students.

Nearly all students have rated the small group sessions as 'effective' or 'very effective' learning experiences, and most of them also regarded the groups as an enjoyable experience; relatively few − usually the anxious students − didn't enjoy them.

From questions designed to evaluate the specific effects of group strategies, students have seen themselves gaining practice from all cognitive categories of test items, although there were always more test items in comprehension and application than in other categories. A majority of the students perceived that they were aided in visual recall while most students indicated that group tests enhanced their skills of comprehension and application. Approximately half of the students considered that the group work helped them in the categories of analysis, synthesis, evaluation, and recall of knowledge.

Students have indicated that they would have attended group sessions even if their written answers to test items were not scored for assessment; these same students also reacted favourably to the practice of using continuous assessment in groups, but some would have preferred a higher rating to be given to this score for overall course assessment.

Responses to specific items in the questionnaires indicated that basic knowledge was acquired by self-instruction in the learning centre and that higher cognitive skills were developed in the groups. With conventional methods of instruction, learning for most students is accomplished largely by subsequent private study.

Internal validity of the ratings given to the SIMIG method has been provided not only by the high percentage of responses (over 98 per cent) across all years but also by comparison of the responses to Table 24 (comparative evaluation of methods used in 1977 across three terms of second-year botany).

CONCLUSIONS: 2 STAFF COMMENT

By P. W. Hattersley PhD, Tutor in Botany 1977-78 (Research Fellow, Taxonomy Unit, Research School of Biological Sciences, ANU Canberra, Australia)

Setting up the material each week for modules was no more complex than for a traditional laboratory. The total volume of material to be organized was greater, reflecting more the greater wealth of teaching materials available to students than any other differences. This was to be expected: the audio-visual learning centre was not only a laboratory in the traditional sense; it provided the total basic material and aids for the self-instruction part of the course.

Group work was a useful experience for students, most of whom preferred this type of discussion. Playing an active role enables a student to appreciate what he actually knows. A student may *think* he knows a certain fact, or appreciates a concept; verbalizing this often reveals shortcomings, or uncertainty, or raises new questions. With time students gain confidence in expressing themselves effectively in public; a desirable spin-off. It took me some time to adapt to the role of a facilitator in the groups; it requires skill, and a full appreciation of the aims and content of each session.

I can see many advantages in structuring content and in modifying and improving material each year. This is 'labour-intensive', compared with what one can 'get away with' in traditional courses, but the method is obviously successful in causing student interactions, and in helping them arrive at their own answers.

Designing the content of group discussions for less factual subjects would probably be simpler: for example, students could be presented with experimental data and asked to deduce which hypotheses are consistent/ inconsistent with the evidence.

9 Application and Costs of SIMIG

APPLICATION TO OTHER DISCIPLINES

The palpable outcomes of the SIMIG method in this longitudinal study are clear, and sufficiently independent of the bias of the investigator to satisfy most sceptics of the worth of innovative teaching methods, particularly the use of audio-visual technology in self-instruction and visual media in peer-group work.

The approach described here is transferable to any subject with a highly visual content. Examples can be suggested from a variety of disciplines such as architecture, history of art, fine arts, statistics, some clinical areas in medicine, dentistry, and veterinary science, as well as most earth and natural sciences. The use of audio-visual technology would be appropriate also for technical subjects, and where manipulative skills are to be learnt. It would not be suitable for courses with philosophical reasoning or subjects such as literature appreciation.

Two criteria might be considered relevant in judging whether the SIMIG approach to group work could be applied to a specific subject. First, would the inclusion of a range of visual material (not necessarily slides) significantly enhance the comprehension of the subject matter, or add a new dimension to learning? Second, would students be encouraged to think critically about the subject matter? This critical approach is required where knowledge is applied to previously unseen examples, or in a different context; in the development of higher cognitive skills; and in teaching problem-solving. If, however, recall of factual material rather than critical thinking is to be emphasized, then there would be less rationale for interaction between students in groups. Undoubtedly, the addition of interactive group discussion would add more impact to some audio-tutorial courses, especially those designed for students above first-year level.

Resistance to change and academic reaction to educational innovation is such as to make highly unlikely the adoption of an entire course by a lecturer at another university. Successful innovations are more likely to be used when potential innovators can put their individual stamp on the product, as in SIMIG. In adapting SIMIG to any suitable discipline, the potentialities of the method are limited only by the imagination of the innovator.

COMPARISON OF COSTS WITH TRADITIONAL METHODS

In these days of financial stringency for higher education it is necessary to ask whether any new strategy for teaching and learning, even if its value is proved, is cost-effective.

Capital Investment

Table 25 indicates that in a course where each student requires a good microscope, a learning centre can be fully equipped for two-thirds of the cost required to accommodate 60 students in a traditional laboratory. Facilities are used for longer periods in the learning centre; 24 microscopes are available for 34 hours each week, whereas 60 students in a lab require 60 microscopes at the same time, for approximately 6 hours. The same number of microscopes (16) are required for demonstrations with both methods.

The learning centre was set up in 1969, in the former library, with a grant of A$6,000, sufficient to:

Purchase hardware: 25 tape-recorders for carrels (open reel); 1 tape-recorder for recording audiotapes, used also as the master in tape duplication; 25 headphones; 2 tape-slide machines; and 60 open-reel tapes.

Purchase pegboard and erect it on existing library tables to make 24 carrels.

Supply electric power to each carrel and link all tape-recorders in the carrels, for tape duplication each week.

	Unit Cost	SIMIG Learning Centre Number of units		Traditional Laboratory Number of units	
MICROSCOPES					
A Grade (carrels)	$400	24	$ 9,600	60	$24,000
B Grade (demonstration)	250	16	4,000	16	4,000
			$13,600		$28,000
HARDWARE					
For Carrels					
Cassette Players	60	24	1,440	–	–
Head phones	15	24	360	–	–
Cassette tapes	200	3	600	–	–
For Tape-Slides					
Projectors	250	3	750	–	–
Cassette players with electronic pulsing for slide change	120	3	360	–	–
Headphones	15	15	225	–	–
Cassette tapes	3	25	75	–	–
For Recording					
Cassette Recorder	250	1	250	–	–
Microphone	60	1	60	–	–
For Seminar Room					
Autofocus Projectors	350	2	700	–	–
			£18,420		£28,000

Table 25
Costs comparison (A$), based on current prices for equipment, in SIMIG learning centre and traditional laboratory.

In 1977, the open-reel recorders were replaced by cassette recorders (which had improved considerably since 1969). Cassette tapes are also much easier to handle and store. Two hundred cassettes were purchased, allowing the audiotape programmes for the eight modules to be duplicated before the course began.

As it is more economical to replace this type of equipment than have it repaired, eventually cassette players (less expensive than cassette recorders) can be installed. A central facility has been established for fast duplication of master cassette tapes.

Technical Assistance

Learning centre Two half-days per week are required for setting up and stripping down the learning centre at beginning and end of the week, when modules are changed. On four mornings per week the centre is checked and fresh plant material supplied (15 minutes).

Laboratory Similar times — perhaps slightly less — are required for setting up and dismantling each week. Whereas, prior to 1969, the laboratory was used for two full days/week (120 students), now it would be in use for one day only.

Staff Contact

This is set out in Table 26. As enrolments have decreased since the centre was set up in 1969, two sets of figures (time in hours) are given: for 70 students (average for 1976 - 78) after the withdrawal of agriculture students due to a change in curriculum; and for 110 students (average for 1969 - 75).

					Contact Time (hours)				
	Lecturer		Tutor		Part-time Demonstrator		Totals		
TRADITIONAL									
Lectures (1 hr)	2		–		–		2		
Laboratory (6 hrs)	6	(12)	6	(12)	36	(54)	48	(78)	
Setting up	–		4		–		4		
Total	8	(14)	10	(16)	36	(54)	54	(84)	
SIMIG									
Groups	8	(6)	6	(5)	–		14	(11)	
Learning Centre	4		7		7	(14)	18	(25)	
Setting up	–		4		–		4		
Total	12		17		7	(14)	36	(40)	

Table 26
Staff contact time with traditional and SIMIG methods: time in hours per week for 70 students (average 1976-78); figures in brackets for 110 students (average 1969-75).

Traditional method Lecturer: two lectures per week; supervisor of 2 x 6 hour laboratory classes (capacity 60) for 110 students or 1 x 6 hour laboratory class for 70 students. Demonstrators: with a staff student ratio of 1:10, a total of 66 hours is required for 110 students, of which the tutor contributes 12 hours; with 70 students a total of 42 hours (tutor 6 hours). Tutor: sets up the microscope demonstrations, and demonstrates in both courses.

SIMIG method Groups: contact time in groups (lecturer and tutor): of 11 x 1 hour for 110 students, 7 x 2 hours for 70 students. Learning centre: open for 34 hours each week (closed for 3 hours each Monday am and Friday pm for setting up and dismantling); no supervisor required for independent study of modules; however, staff qualified to demonstrate (when required) on duty in the centre for 27 hours each week (110 students) or 18 hours each week (70 students); technical staff used in lunch-hour periods with the larger classes.

Overall − staff contact time With 110 students, there was much less overall contact time with SIMIG (43 hours) than with traditional teaching (84 hours). Most of this was by part-time demonstrators (54 hours) and the overall man-hours spent in the two labs was 78 hours. Even with 70 students (as in 1976 - 78), more staff:student contact time would have been required with traditional teaching. Moreover, the time spent by the lecturer and tutor in groups is almost equivalent to time spent in the learning centre.

Preparation of Course Material

The initial preparation of course material for SIMIG takes a great deal of time, far longer, in my experience, than the writing of a course of lectures and the preparation of materials for traditional lab work, and representing an unavoidable investment of time and energy for the staff concerned (see Appendix C: Guidelines for Preparing Audio-visual Self-instructional Units).

10 The Author's Reflections on SIMIG

INTRODUCTION

Let me now rescue readers from the jungle of data through which they have (I hope) successfully struggled; to come back to my opening sentence: the maxim given to teachers by Comenius three centuries ago. Of course there have been hundreds of schemes to follow his maxim; SIMIG, or self-instruction by modules and interactive groups, is only one more of these schemes. Its scope is limited but within that scope I think I have demonstrated, by analysing records of test scores and examinations, that it fulfils Comenius's maxim: students learn more, the tutor teaches less.

This book is a personal account of my own experiences, not a treatise. So I shall not embark on a comparative study of all the other schemes devised by those I call disciples of Comenius. But a review of the foundations on which SIMIG was built should be put into perspective with other views on innovative teaching methods in higher education.

Universities are an invention of the Middle Ages, when the authority of the teacher was paramount. Even in the nineteenth century a Cambridge academic (Isaac Todhunter) could condemn the idea of illustrating science by experiments: students, he thought, should be prepared to accept the teacher's word and not require visual demonstrations (Ashby 1958, p.42). Slowly, under the influence of teachers like T. H. Huxley, the student was encouraged to question authority. As Eric Ashby has put it, the student must first learn orthodoxy, then the art of dissent from orthodoxy (Ashby 1974, p.23). The tutorial system as practised in Oxford and Cambridge and the seminar system as practised in Germany were nineteenth-century products of the disciples of Comenius; in modern jargon, they were innovative techniques. They were, however, too expensive for the Scottish-type universities which became models for universities in Australia; here, mass-lectures and mass-practical classes had to remain the common style of teaching.

It is only since the Second World War that technology has been applied to education. Language laboratories, film strips, combinations of slides and tapes, programmed instruction, teaching machines: all generated a new euphoria for innovation. A Fund for the Advancement of Education in the USA put millions of dollars into experiments with these gadgets. The chief lesson learnt from it all was that there is a modest place for technology in education, but the quality of education still depends upon the 'software' –

the intellectual contribution put into the use of gadgets – and not upon the 'hardware'.

There were two basic problems to be solved. What material do you put into the tape in the language laboratory, the audiotape and the tape-slide in the biology laboratory, the film in the seminar, the diagrams, projected slides, and specimens used to enrich the course? Secondly, how do you elicit the response of students to these mechanized sources of information, get students to reflect on the material, to use it for reasoning, to integrate it into the whole discipline of which it is only a part? In a word, how can the student be *liberated* from the teacher and obliged to become *independent* or *autonomous*? All the innovations: self-pacing, self-instruction, small group learning, peer-group learning, peer tutoring, are attempts to solve these two basic problems. SIMIG is just one such attempt.

DISCIPLES OF COMENIUS
The main innovations made by others, and to which I am indebted, are: the audio-tutorial system of self-instruction, self-pacing and mastery learning, and small group discussion. These are described and discussed under the appropriate sections.

The Audio-Tutorial System
Postlethwait (1964, 1969) is the innovator of the audio-tutorial (A-T) system, first used in subjects requiring laboratory work, and conceived to provide an environment which actively involved the learner. He first used remedial audiotapes and other manipulative and visual materials in 1961, at Purdue University, Indiana, for selected students (lacking suitable backgrounds) enrolled in first-year botany. The method was so successful that by 1963 he had converted the fourteen-week semester of traditional teaching for 300 students to the A-T method; by 1968 600 students had enrolled in this elective course. The method is centred on self-instruction and independent study in a carrel (booth) with the appropriate hardware and audiotapes to guide the student through various types of learning activities. The programme is linear (not branching), and alternates listening with examining relevant laboratory materials, experimenting, reading and observation of demonstrations set up in other parts of the learning centre. Visual aids, a study guide and the necessary materials are in the carrel, while other audio-visual equipment, such as film loops, are shared between two or more carrels. The learning centre is open all day, students choose their own study times, and are self-paced within the constraint that the unit of study is changed each week. Demonstrators are always available to assist students with difficulties.

Associated with this independent study session is the 'small assembly' – groups of ten or so students who meet with a tutor once a week for the 'integrated quiz session' on the completed programme. Here, oral quizzing with a tutor is followed by a written quiz paper, later marked by the tutor. General assembly sessions to view a film or attend a guest lecture are for the whole class. Additional assignments or research projects may be undertaken for extra credit. Course assessment includes scores from weekly quizzes, assignments, projects and a final examination.

The self-instructional modules of SIMIG utilize all the features of carrel study (see Chapter 2) but the audiotapes are longer, and the programmes more sophisticated than is usual for general biology. Tape-slides are used, but not film loops. More and different emphasis is placed on group work (Chapters 3, 6, 7), and, apart from the first scheduled lecture slot, the whole class does not meet together for any activities.

In a review of A-T instruction, Fisher and MacWhinney note that the method has been applied to many disciplines other than biology at college level: twenty-four science subjects and twelve non-science. The latter included such diverse subjects as industrial engineering, accounting, algebra, and academic instruction for the US Air Force. This last use is interesting, in view of the fact that the British Royal Air Force have found an integrated approach more effective than instruction through un-integrated films and lectures.

A-T courses that 'fade away' do so for a variety of reasons: lack of educational expertise or inexperience in the techniques of making audiotapes for example; insufficient technical assistance or shoddy hardware; or more usually faculty resistance to innovation — especially noticeable after the innovator has departed.

Self-pacing and Mastery Learning
Particularly in the last two decades, the notion of mastery learning has been pursued, and effective strategies for its use have been developed. These involve self-pacing and self-instruction, flexibility of timetabling and of testing, for to achieve mastery of a learning task, ie performance at a prescribed level, some students need to return for re-testing several times.

Carroll (1963) provided a useful mastery learning model for schools. Briefly, he contended that the degree of learning was a function of the ratio of the time spent to the time needed to learn a task to some specified level. If a student spends the amount of time he requires — and this varies with the individual — he will attain the designated level of mastery. Bloom (1968) transformed Carroll's conceptual model (a refinement of the above) into an effective working model for mastery learning. Bloom argued that if the aptitudes of students for a subject were normally distributed then achievement also would be normally distributed, providing instruction was uniform in quality and the time allowed was the same for each student. Conversely, achievement at end of course would have a skewed distribution — with the majority achieving mastery — if instruction were optimal in quality and allowed each individual the learning time required. With mastery learning, the assumption is that given enough time, and appropriate instruction, almost all students can attain mastery, in the sense in which Bloom uses the word.

In the audio-tutorial system (and in SIMIG), self-pacing for each unit is limited to within one week, followed by the weekly group sessions. Irrespective of the level of attainment in the attendant assessment tests, all students proceed at the same time to the next unit of study; so mastery learning can be encouraged in A-T and SIMIG courses, but cannot be (so to speak) 'guaranteed'. Nevertheless, each student's performance is matched against a standard (as with par in golf) not against the performance of his peers.

To implement the idea of mastery learning, Postlethwait adapted the A-T approach in developing *minicourses* (Postlethwait and Russell 1971; Hurst and Postlethwait 1971). A minicourse is a short, self-contained instructional package (audiotape and portable materials) for use in a carrel, in the library or at home. Whereas A-T units are too large and inflexible to allow *repetition* of study, necessary for re-testing and mastery learning, the design of the portable minicourse does allow repetition of any or all segments — until an acceptable level of performance is attained.

An entirely different approach to mastery learning, to teach general psychology, was developed by Keller (1968). His strategy for mastery learning was to use the principles of reinforcement theory, with student tutors (who had recently completed the course) providing the amount and type of reinforcement required by individual students.

Keller's personalized system of instruction (PSI) is a major innovation in college teaching in the USA, and has been used successfully elsewhere, particularly in chemistry, physics, mathematics, engineering, psychology, and some social and life sciences. PSI courses are characterized by: (1) mastery learning, (2) self-pacing, (3) student tutors, (4) printed 'hand-outs' to direct students' learning (a study plan and references to text books), (5) occasional lectures for stimulation/motivation, (6) personal attention/tutoring whenever required, and (7) tests or quizzes, repeated without penalty, to demonstrate mastery of each unit.

At the University of Sydney, as in many other universities, existing constraints preclude testing for mastery; courses must be contained within the term/semester; science subjects usually have fairly stringent weekly schedules; self-pacing is not encouraged; students are expected to attend lectures and labs at specified times; and assessment tests (continuing or final examinations) are usually end of semester/term or end of year fixtures. Nevertheless, teaching for mastery — at a realistic level — even in traditional universities, can properly be a goal for teachers and a challenge to those students who all too readily accept the notion that 'passing' a subject is good enough.

Small Group Discussion

I do not intend to review the extensive literature of the techniques of small group discussion in higher education. There was no model in the literature for the design of the new type of SIMIG group (described on pp. 23 - 27) introduced in 1972.

I had the good fortune, in 1973, to meet Jane Abercrombie, a visitor to the University of Sydney, and later I attended some of her groups in the Bartlett School of Architecture, at University College London. Subsequently I was invited to join a few sessions of the group meetings for teachers, covered by the series reported in her book *Talking to Learn* (1978). Her example greatly influenced my role as a group tutor in stimulating peer interaction, and demonstrated the importance of the introductory group session designed to 'break the ice'.

Abercrombie developed a discussion technique for training in observation and reasoning (Johnson 1950, 1953; Abercrombie 1960), to help preclinical medical students to observe accurately and comprehensively and to draw reasonable conclusions from their observations. At first she described this as 'free' group discussion and later as 'associative' discussion (Abercrombie 1970).

There are very obvious differences between Abercrombie's 'associative' discussion and the structured discussion of SIMIG groups — organized by specific questions, restricted by time, and therefore keeping close to the point. Nonetheless, the aim of fostering critical thinking is common to both discussion groups, so is learning from one another by exposing the differences which exist in the receipt of information from a visual pattern (slides or radiographs), and involving the processes of selection and interpretation.

The following extracts from Abercrombie's *Anatomy of Judgement* (1969 edition) illustrate that the underlying motives in both types of group discussion have something in common.

'In the discussion technique of teaching, the student learns by comparing his observation with those of ten or so of his peers. He compares not only the results, but how the results were arrived at.' (p. 19)

'Before each discussion group began, the students worked individually at an exercise which served as a basis for the discussion. ... The particular type of group discussion envisaged was not intended to provide a group solution to a problem; the group was not a team in the sense that a specific job had to be done in co-operation. ... The aim was to provide a medium (the group discussion) in which each individual could learn about his own reactions. The intention was that each student should write down his own spontaneous reactions to a given stimulus (eg report of an experiment) in preparation for this.' (pp. 83-84)

'In free group discussion, the students are presented with the same information (eg two radiographs or an account of an experiment), but it soon becomes clear that they do not extract the same information from it, and learning depends on the fact that each extracts something different. Discussion of the differences of their reactions involves discovering not only what factors influenced the kind of selection they made from the information presented, but it also involves exploring their own store of information.' (p. 79)

The *structure* of SIMIG groups avoids many of the difficulties experienced by others in group work: perhaps the two most frequently reported difficulties being irregular attendance and problems of participation (see Rudduck 1978, pp. 12-20). Attendance is mandatory in SIMIG groups, and it includes assessment. Problems of participation are minimized in SIMIG groups by the following strategies: (1) all members have sufficient prior knowledge (from module study) to take part in discussion; (2) the question paper provides a secure framework for discussion; (3) group members act on the suggestion that they take turns in providing the first responses to questions, by reading their own written answers to the group; (4) assessment is by written answers, no subjective assessment is made of contributions to open discussions, so frankness and spontaneity are encouraged; and (5) self-assessment, ie provisional marking of their own answers encourages discussion by defending written answers.

SUMMARY OF SIMIG TECHNIQUES
The virtue of SIMIG is that it combines two well tried techniques:

self-instruction, using the A-T format, with a degree of self-pacing, and a very carefully organized style of small group discussion, monitored by weekly assessments and culminating in a final examination. The main features of the technique can be outlined under the heads: self-instruction by modules; group discussions; weekly assessment in groups; and final examination.

Self-instruction by Modules
This promotes effective learning in the following ways:
>*The multi-media learning centre* combines a variety of learning resources, which in traditional teaching are segregated in the library, laboratory or lecture theatre. Open access allows flexible study times.
>
>*Self-pacing* helps to accommodate the different backgrounds and aptitudes of learners. The individual student determines the time he is prepared to spend on the module each week.
>
>*Self-instructional materials* (the printed study guide and audio-tape) give adequate instructions for their use, and are designed to guide the student through a series of sequential learning tasks.
>
>*Students* participate at all stages of independent study. In the linear programme, students with special interest in the subject can make digressions using optional material provided. There is a limited degree of choice in selecting from the learning activities those which best suit the individual (eg a few students have tried to work without the audiotape).
>
>*Self-assessment* during independent study is provided by self-quizzes in the study guide; the suggested answers may be discussed with other students or the demonstrator. By viewing the tape-slide summary on completion of study, the student can assess his comprehension of the overall content of the module.

Group Discussions
Self-instruction promotes autonomous learning, but students are challenged in the groups to exercise a range of intellectual skills, instead of placing undue emphasis on recall of factual knowledge. Rather than just building on the information acquired individually in module study, in group discussion basic concepts are reinforced, misconceptions removed and students are confronted with applying knowledge and with simple problems they are obliged to solve. Presentation of specific questions with slides providing visual cues, commitment to paper of each individual's responses, and discussion on those written comments further encourages self-reliance in learning.

Weekly Assessment in Groups
Formative evaluation by so-called 'diagnostic progress tests' are usually ungraded. But I deliberately used weekly tests in SIMIG groups for continuing assessment, making attendance mandatory. Only those questions requiring written responses were scored. Others, used for discussion only, militated against the build-up of anxiety levels for anxious students.

The tests were designed as an integral part of the teaching-learning process; administered on completion of each module, they assessed the knowledge and skills each student had or had not learned. They were especially useful because material used in early modules forms the basis for learning in subsequent ones.

Weekly tests also provided feedback essential to the individual for monitoring his own progress; probably a synergistic effect resulted from each student giving a provisional mark to his own test paper.

Final Examinations

A three-hour, 'open book' examination, given at the end of the course was weighted equally with weekly test scores for course assessment. The format of the examination — short-answer questions requiring investigation of practical material — was retained throughout the period of study, though the content became more demanding by increasing the proportion of problem questions from 26 per cent in 1971 (when they were introduced) to 80 per cent in 1978.

Examination papers were not published, so some questions were retained with minor alterations, providing a relevant basis for comparison of performance, and for criterion testing of problems.

EVALUATION OF STUDENT LEARNING FROM ASSESSMENT RESULTS

From the great amount of detail emerging from the monitoring of this ten-year study, outstanding results (from Chapters 4-7) are summarized under the heads: assessment by weekly tests, assessment by final examination.

Assessment by Weekly Tests

1   Within each of the four cohorts analysed (1975-78) *mean performance* increased by 10 per cent during the first six weeks of tests on modules (Table 11).
2   *Frequency distributions of test scores* changed from 'normal' in the first week to negatively skewed (ie in the direction of better performance) by the fifth week (Table 12).
3   Over the six weeks, more students in each cohort attained *mastery* (80%) and fewer *failed* (Table 12).
4   The improvement in mean performance of test scores within cohorts is not related to *time spent in self-instruction*: over the six weeks there was no increase in mean time spent on module study (Table 13).
5   Students achieving *mastery level* spent on average more time in self-instruction than those achieving all other levels of performance (Table 14).
6   For a high proportion of individuals, *performance* in weekly tests on modules was not related to time spent in self-instruction (Table 15).
7   From the study of individual learning profiles, the only category of performance which changed significantly across weeks was the profile of *performance in short-chain problems* (p. 95).
8   Students classified as Type I (the most competent) and Type II (average to fair) maintained their *performance levels* from high entry behaviours, without significant change. Type III students (mediocre at entry) showed significant change in performance, attaining relatively high levels of competence from low entry scores (Figs. 16, 17).

9   Type III students were primarily responsible for the change in *frequency distributions* from normal in the first week to negatively skewed in the fifth week (Fig. 18).

10 Type III students derived most *benefit from SIMIG*, particularly Type IIIA, who sustained their level of performance in final examination. Type I students (and a few Type II individuals) who surpassed their predicted score in examination also benefited (p. 88).

11 Students with Type I and Type IIIA profiles generally averaged more *time in module study* than all other types (Table 18).

Assessment by Final Examinations

1   From 1968-1978 there was an improvement in *overall examination performance*. Phases of improvement and fluctuations were related to fortuitous variation in ability of cohorts, to the proportion of problems in examination, and to changes in teaching method (Fig. 4).

2   The *overall failure* rate decreased from 16 per cent in 1968 to 3 per cent in 1980 (Table 6).

3   The percentages of students gaining *mastery* (80%) in examination improved across the whole sample (>1,000) but fluctuated between cohorts according to the above variables. Marked increases were related to changes in teaching methods: from traditional in 1968 (2 per cent mastery) to self-instruction(SIM) in 1969 (22 per cent mastery); from 1971 (16 per cent) to 1972 (29 per cent) with the introduction of slide-based group work (SIMIG); from 1974 (12 per cent) to 1975 (25 per cent), and from 1975 to 1977 (40 per cent) with improvements in group work from 1974 (Table 6).

4   The evolution from normal *frequency distribution curves of examination scores*, typical of 1965-1968 with traditional teaching, to negatively skewed distribution in 1969, and thereafter, 'correlates' with the introduction of systematic self-instruction (SIM) (Fig. 5).

5   From 1974, *frequency distribution of overall examination scores* became increasingly skewed, simultaneously with the increase in percentage students achieving mastery (Figs. 7, 8).

6   In 1977 and 1978 (with 76 per cent and 80 per cent problems in examination) the top portion of the *negative skew split and became bimodal*, effectively separating 40 per cent of the 1977 cohort, and 31 per cent of the 1978 cohort who had attained overall mastery in examination (Fig. 9).

7   From 1971-78 there was an improvement in *performance of problem questions*, as itemized below:

   a   A significant increase in the percentage of students *passing problems* (p. 50).

   b   An increase in the *'modes' of frequency distribution scores* of problems − for comparable samples − from decile groupings of 60-69 per cent in 1974, and 70-79 per cent in 1975, to 80-89 per cent in 1977 (Fig. 10, Table 7).

   c   An increase in the percentage of students gaining *mastery in overall scores in problems*, from 2 per cent in 1974 to 46 per cent in 1977 (22 per cent in 1978 with a cohort of lesser ability). The percentage *failing problems* also decreased, from 75 per cent in 1971 to 4 per cent in 1977 and 1978 (Fig. 11).

        d A significant increase at mastery level in *performance in five individual problems* from 1974-77 (Table 8).

8 Improvements in performance at mastery level in individual problems, over cohorts from 1974-77, have been correlated with changes in *group teaching strategies* and increases in specific media components used in groups, viz. number of slide transparencies, and number of questions testing higher order cognitive skills (Table 9, Figure 12).

9 Improvement in *overall examination performance* from 1975-78 was not related to time spent in self-instruction of modules: there was no increase in mean time spent over this period (Table 10).

10 *Mean time spent by students attaining mastery* was significantly greater than for all other grades (Table 10). This relationship is by no means universal; for a high proportion of individuals, performance is not related to time spent (see also assessment in weekly tests, items 4-6).

11 From the *learning profiles*, some predictions could be made about subsequent performance in examination:

        a For about 60 per cent of each cohort *examination performance* could be predicted from individual learning profiles, to within 5% of the actual examination score (Table 16).

        b It was not performance in problems in weekly tests by itself which predicted overall examination performance, but *test scores in 'combined skills'*. This is not surprising, for it was the purpose of summative assessment in SIMIG to test students' capacity to combine knowledge with the skills of comprehension, application, and 'creative' thinking acquired during the course (p. 95).

        c The majority of those most accurately predicted were among Types II and IIIA. Type I usually surpassed their *predicted scores*, and Type IIIB rarely attained those predicted (p. 87).

12 Not only did the *students who performed well* throughout the course (Type I) achieve mastery, but so also did some of those mediocre students who had entered the course with low scores in weekly tests (Type IIIA) improve steadily across the seven weeks, then maintain their improved levels in examination (Fig. 19).

13 A majority of Type I students gained both *overall mastery* in examination and *mastery in problems*, while Type IIIA achieved mastery on more problems that Type II. A considerably higher percentage of students with profile types I and IIIA gained mastery in 1977 (Table 17).

CONCLUSIONS: VERDICT ON SIMIG

The following quotation from the preface to the *Handbook on Formative and Summative Evaluation of Student Learning* (Bloom, Hastings and Madaus 1971) might well apply to the study reported here: 'Properly used, evaluation should enable teachers to make marked improvements in their students' learning. It is the improvement of student learning which is the central concern of this book.'

In the evolution of the SIMIG method, analysis of process and end results has demonstrated that evaluation of weekly assessment tests and assessment by final examination have been used consistently, year by year, to improve students' learning.

As new challenges arose, I had to make new responses; most of these were in the manipulation of media and refinements of techniques used in group discussions. Effective changes in teaching techniques were reflected in four distinct phases of improvement in examination performance at mastery level: between the pairs of cohorts 1968/1969, 1971/1972, 1974/1975 and 1975/1977 (pp. 48, 60).

With the changeover in 1969 from teaching plant anatomy by lectures and laboratory classes to self-instruction by modules (SIM), a variety of features — typical of audio-tutorial methods in general — contributed to the overall improvement in the 1969 examination results. Explicit statements of objectives, independent study with self-pacing and choice of study times, were absent from the previous traditional method. Undoubtedly, the most effective changes in teaching learning techniques were: the integration by the audiotape — complemented by the study guide — of laboratory experience with theoretical aspects; the structure of a sequential series of learning activities to accomplish the stated objectives; incorporation at appropriate intervals of feedback from self-quizzes to test comprehension; and the efficient use of audio-visual in conjunction with printed media.

Central to the academic study was the participation demanded by the audiotape, with independent study requiring individuals to decide both the depth at which the material was to be covered and the time they were prepared to spend in self-instruction.

The introduction of problem questions in the 1971 examination presented a challenge which could not be met by the average student. At this stage I was able to introduce the new type of group discussion which distinguishes SIMIG from the classical A-T approach (p. 7). For this it was necessary to have a seminar room equipped with remote-control slide projection. This became available in 1972, by which time I had made and collected sufficient slide transparencies to use with a printed question paper. Small group discussions had always been an integral part of the teaching method, but, for this factual and highly visual subject, their effectiveness as a learning experience had been limited — until 1972 — by the lack of suitable visual material for discussion.

From 1972 to 1978 cognitive demand of test items used in group discussions was gradually increased (Fig. 1), resulting in a greater focus on the separate skills required for solving anatomical problems. The number of slides used in group sessions was also increased (Table 1), resulting in familiarity with a greater variety of examples. Longer group sessions (from 1976) resulted in an increase in time spent on discussion, and over this period of time, tutors, including myself, became more familiar and more adept with the part they played in this style of teaching. Accompanying these changes (pp. 60, 64) there had been a decrease in failure rate and a significant improvement in ability to solve examination problems, as judged by performance of cohorts from 1974 to 1977 (Tables 7, 8).

The proportion of problems in examination (an index of difficulty — (p. 43) had also been increased over this period (Fig. 3). On the assumption that problem-solving is some measure of critical thinking in this discipline, it can be concluded that the changes in style of instruction had improved the individual skills of students working within the group (p. 64). Doubtless many factors, not all quantified (p. 76), contributed to this improvement.

Nonetheless, in the analysis of performance in individual examination problems, it has been possible to isolate the effect of two variables — the number of discussion items testing higher cognitive skills, and the number of slides (visual examples) — on significant improvements in performance at mastery level (p. 60).

The magnitude of the effect of reinforcing visual recall by slide transparencies was demonstrated by one critical experiment — the only one deliberately devised. Particular slide transparencies relevant to one examination problem were removed from the group sessions in one year (1975) and re-instated in the following two years. A significant decrease in performance at mastery level in 1975 was followed by a return to the levels of mastery in 1976/77 previously established for 1974 (p. 61).

To confirm that the refinements — in group techniques and use of media — created the better performance, it was necessary to examine other possible causes, eg that over the weeks of each course, and over years, more time was spent in self-instruction. Mean time spent in self-instruction of modules by successive cohorts from 1975-78 did not increase, thus providing unequivocal evidence that time did not account for the improvement in examination performance from 1975-78 (p. 64). Within each cohort, there was no increase in mean time spent over weeks, again showing that the 10% increase in weekly test scores recorded for each cohort (p. 73) was not related to time.

In both types of assessment, the significant difference between mean time spent by students attaining mastery level and time spent by students in all other grades is interpreted as a reflection of the type of student; the relationship was by no means universal; for most individuals, performance is independent of time (pp. 64 - 75).

No attempt was made in SIMIG groups to teach a strategy for solving a particular problem, and then to test an analogous (transfer) problem in examination. Perusal of one complex problem question used in examination and the multiple steps required for its solution (Notes 12 and 13, pp. 55 and 56) show that this is not a straight transfer problem for which the strategies are learned in the relevant group session (Note 7, p. 35). However, the basic anatomical concepts and rules necessary for solution of this and any other examination problem were discussed (and tested) in groups, as were all the other objectives for each module.

In group discussions the students learn from one another. For at least half the time in the group sessions they can discuss problems among themselves as they respond to each item presented to them. This is an essential feature in the educational strategy of SIMIG. The tutor's role is to create among students, as they discuss, the atmosphere of a 'game'; they are provoked into competing with ideas and taking risks.

At no time during this study were students manipulated to fit into a research project; nor have they been guinea pigs in experimental and control groups. Over the years they have willingly co-operated in their personal evaluation of SIMIG, particularly in the period 1976-78 (for the research on learning profiles) by responding to many more questionnaires than they are usually requested to for this course. Perhaps this response indicated their recognition of the research as identical in its interests with the teaching.

The learning profiles of individual students throw light on the response of students to challenges presented by group work. The profiles may be regarded as indicators of intellectual development. Experience in the groups has undoubtedly contributed to the development of individuals with Profile Type III. The greatest improvement in the development of problem-solving skills was shown by students with Type IIIA profiles, characterized by low entry scores in this category of test items. Individuals who had high entry scores for problems (Type I) and maintained this level may also have improved.

The high proportion of cohorts gaining overall mastery in examination and the mix of students — Type I, II, IIIA — are perhaps the criteria which should be used to evaluate the efficacy of the SIMIG method, for they demonstrate that the techniques and materials used improved the performance of average and mediocre students sufficiently for them to demonstrate mastery in an examination which is a rigorous test of their knowledge and skills.

The study reported here can be summarized very briefly: as the method of teaching and learning in groups was refined, more students mastered the content and fewer failed.

The most controversial conclusion that emerges from the data presented is that distribution curves of weekly test scores became negatively skewed over the duration of the course, and that the distribution curves for the scores of final examinations are negatively skewed too; in the terminology of learning for mastery, a larger majority of students gained mastery of the content — ie scored 80% or more in the examination — than they would have done under a conventional system. This conclusion offends those academics/educators who have become convinced that examination scores should conform to a normal distribution: in effect that only a minority of students — perhaps 10 per cent — can 'learn' (as inferred by a set criterion for satisfactory performance) what we teach. Indeed so strongly is this belief held that some examining bodies, even in élite universities, actually modify the marks of the examiners to make the overall scores fit such a curve.

'The normal curve is not sacred. It describes the outcome of a random process. Since education is a purposeful activity in which we seek to have students learn what we teach, the achievement distribution should be very different from the normal curve if our instruction is effective. In fact, our educational efforts may be said to be *unsuccessful* to the extent that student achievement is normally distributed' (Bloom 1971, p.49).

It is not surprising that this process of grading on a normal curve has been challenged (Bloom 1968; Block et al. 1971) and that new methods of instruction using mastery learning techniques have been initiated, eg Keller (1968) and Postlethwait and Russell (1971). The process not only determines academic goals and limits the aspirations of both students and teachers, but more importantly it reduces students' motivation for learning and damages self-confidence. To assume that examination scores must always fall on a normal distribution curve would be to deny that any innovation in teaching could ever be an improvement: that is why I believe that the assumption is not only misguided; it is also a counsel of despair. And the teacher who despairs has no claim to belong to the tradition set by Comenius.

Appendix A

Records and Tests

TIME AND PERFORMANCE RECORDS

Two record cards, with photographs, were kept for every student: one for time spent in module study in the learning centre; and one for performance in weekly test items, to which the examination score was added later.

Time Records

Individual time records were on attendance cards, filed in the learning centre. Total time spent each week, ie on each module, was calculated from the one or more entries made on an attendance card for each visit. Times were entered routinely on arrival and departure from the learning centre, when students were required to place (or remove) their cards in (or from) a wall rack (with slots to correspond to carrels), thus indicating which carrels were in use at any particular time. These records provided the estimated time spent in independent study per module.

Steffen (1971, p. 78), in a study of observer-reported versus student-reported laboratory attendance times, concluded that, despite their potential for inaccuracy, student-reported time records were the most economical method ($r = .77$). Our own observations for this course have indicated that very little attendance time was not actual working time.

Analysis of these time records showed that the absolute range was from three to eight hours per week (ie per module), although most students averaged the recommended time of approximately five hours.

Performance Records

Individual scores for weekly tests on modules were entered on a second set of cards, filed in the seminar room where all group meetings were held. Scores were recorded according to the cognitive demand of items in: (i) recall of knowledge, (ii) comprehension, (iii) application, (iv) simple problem-solving – requiring knowledge and skills of the previous categories, plus additional components from the skills of analysis and/or evaluation based on Bloom (1956) – see Chapter 4.

Weekly Tests used in Performance Analysis

As discussion and weekly tests on modules were held in the week following independent study of each module, it was possible to schedule only eight discussion groups in the nine-week term. Of these, scores from seven weekly tests were available for analysis (Chapter 7) of each individual's performance. In the other discussion group, students presented (oral) reports to their own group on their individually assigned anatomy project (substituting for a module in the seventh week of term). The assessment mark, given for the written report, was therefore not comparable.

In the analysis of time spent in module study in relation to performance levels in weekly tests (as in Chapter 5) only six modules were strictly comparable for time. In the last week of term, penultimate to the regular university term exams (and including the Final for this course), time spent in module study was not consistent with previous weeks: some students spent more time than usual, as they revised other modules during the week, while others spent less than usual time, depending on subject priorities for examination.

TESTS ADMINISTERED
Course Assessment
Tests used for summative assessment by final examination, and weekly tests in group sessions, used for continuing (formative) assessment, are discussed in Chapters 3, 4, 6 and 7. They were equally weighted (from 1972) for overall course assessment.

Reference Test
A multiple choice test (mcq) given immediately before and after the course (ie pre- and post-test) was used as a reference test. This mcq test has been used since 1974 and was the basis of an attrition study by further administrations six and twelve months after the completion of the course (see Appendix B: Attrition).

The reference test consisted of eleven multiple choice questions – classified as comprehension – used with microscope slides. Pre-test and post-test results are summarized in Table 3.

The State/Trait Anxiety Inventory (STAI)
The State/Trait Anxiety Inventory (STAI) test was supplied under licence from the Consulting Psychologists Press, Inc., Palo Alto, California, USA. Two forms were administered to provide measures of general anxiety ('trait'), compared with that induced by final examination ('state'). Whereas the 'trait' test was given in the sixth group meeting, the 'state' test was administered in the examination room, prior to commencement. (All students complied with this request.)

The difference between normalized scores in both forms of the test questionnaire indicated the effect of examination on anxiety levels (variable for profile types), and the relationship between general anxiety levels and other student attributes or performance variables (also evident between profile types – see Chapter 7).

ETS Hidden Figures Test
The Hidden Figures Test, Form CF-1 (Rev.) was supplied under licence from the Educational Testing Service, Princeton, NJ, USA. It was used from 1976 to 1978 as a test for field independence/field dependence (a visual skill). This test indicates ability to discriminate figure from ground; those

who can readily discern shapes within the whole are referred to as field-independent while those who view the field as a whole are field-dependent. Results from this test suggested, not unexpectedly, that performance in plant anatomy was influenced by visual skills.

Banks' Learning Styles Test

Banks' Learning Styles Test was taken from 'An Investigation of the Interactions of Learning Styles and Types of Learning Experiences in Vocational and Technical Education', by John C. Banks (June, 1973) from the University of Wisconsin (Stout), Menemonie, Wisc., USA. This test, which estimates two continua of style — structured or unstructured and concrete or abstract — was routinely administered in the first and seventh week of the course. In the questionnaire, statements describing a variety of activities used to learn skills and obtain knowledge, are responded to (in five categories) on the basis of the value of each item to the individual as a learning activity. Specific learning preferences on the continua (evaluated from scores on twenty-two items) indicate whether an individual student prefers his material presented in a structured or unstructured way and whether it is coded in abstract (symbolic) or concrete terms.

The test was administered pre- and post-instruction from 1976 to 1978 to determine whether the teaching itself was effective in another (non-cognitive) mode — see Chapter 7.

Manipulative Skills Test

As lack of manipulative skill in the preparation of microscope slides (from fresh material) could adversely affect a student's examination performance (in interpreting structure) a manipulative skills test was used from 1976-78. The test involved the cutting, staining, mounting and presentation of a microscope slide. It was applied the first time students were required to make their own sections of plant material (second module, second week) and in the final examination ten weeks later.

QUESTIONNAIRES ON THE COURSE

In all years, questionnaires were given to students from which information was obtained about their attitudes to aspects of courses either completed or about to begin. Responses were scored on a 5-point scale (unless stated otherwise) and were abstracted and analysed by a standardized procedure whereby all were equally weighted and converted to percentages.

The Course Introductory Questionnaire

The introductory questionnaire provided information about the students' prior experience, vocational interest, course and subject expectancy, subject choice (ie whether biology was a first preference, or enrolment was determined by other factors).

The Course Evaluation Questionnaire (CEQ)

The evaluation questionnaire canvassed all aspects of the course, but recently placed emphasis on teaching-learning as experienced in the small groups of the SIMIG method, with particular reference to the students' perceived objectives of the group sessions.

STATISTICAL METHODOLOGY

Standard parametric (t) and non-parametric (Wilcoxon) tests of difference between years on different parameters were carried out. For data which involved proportions of students at particular levels of performance, differences were analysed using the normal approximation, ie the z statistic: the standard normal variate calculated as regression coefficient divided by the standard error. Where differences across three or more years were investigated, monotonic trend analysis or Chi squared (x^2) for frequency data, corrected for different sample sizes, were used. Rank correlation coefficients were calculated using Spearman's rho where the variance estimates were not homogeneous. Reliability of tests was estimated by Cronbach's α and/or Kuder-Richardson methods — KR_{20} or KR_{21} — depending on the scoring of each assessment. Multiple linear regressions and analyses of variance were computed.

COURSE ORGANIZATION

Course Records

Copies of examination papers and weekly test papers, plus all materials used, have been kept, together with point score marking systems for the examination questions, and complete records of slides used in weekly tests. Retrospective analyses were made from these records. Additionally, examination scripts for all students in each cohort from 1968-78 were kept, allowing analysis of point score marking and comparisons of performance in individual questions across years.

Module Materials

Each module is packaged with twenty-six sets of carrel photomicrographs and boxes of microscope slides. Demonstration material is also filed for each module. Materials in the learning centre are dismantled every Friday afternoon and set up for the next module on Monday morning. Housekeeping for modular instruction is therefore similar to laboratory preparation for classes, but usually with much more demonstration material.

Group Materials

Weekly test papers are xeroxed prior to the beginning of the course, and slides are kept in sequence in slide folders or cartridges.

Tape-Recordings

The University of Sydney has only recently acquired a centre for audio-visual services and recordings, so all master tapes were originally recorded in my own study at home. Subsequently, the seminar room (fairly soundproof) was used, especially when two voices were introduced in the audiotape recordings. Duplication of tapes in situ in the learning centre was accomplished by linking all the carrel tape-decks to the master. In 1977, after cassette tape-decks replaced the open-reel machines, a sufficient number of cassettes were purchased and could be recorded for the whole course, thus avoiding tape duplication each week.

Appendix B

Attrition

The efficacy of teaching-learning may be considered both in terms of what is learned in the short term and what is remembered in the long term. One measure of immediate learning is by a reference test (see Appendix A: Records and Tests, and Chapter 4, Table 3) given on completion of the course (post-test) compared with the same test given before the course (pre-test). Retention may then be estimated by a delayed post-test at various time intervals. The difference between the scores obtained on these post-tests (attrition) represents loss of knowledge of the subject matter of the course.

A measure of attrition was carried out using the responses obtained from the reference test given six and twelve months after the course. Two methods of analysis were carried out. A simple loss analysis comparing the loss of performance with time over the two six-monthly periods, and a two-way analysis of variance with repeated measures, which allowed all data (irrespective of degree of completeness) to be included. Apart from the effect of time on correct responses ($P<0.001$) there were no other significant findings.

Attrition results, summarized in Table 27, are shown (C) as change in overall percentage performance giving a loss of 13 per cent for the first six months and a further 11 per cent for the period of six to twelve months. More usually, attrition can be expressed as a percentage loss in performance, ie 17 per cent after six months or 32 per cent after twelve months. This equates post-test performance as 100 per cent, ie the maximum level of student achievement relative to which subsequent loss is measured.

In terms of overall performance, this attrition rate is comparable to that observed for medical students in anatomy (Blunt and Blizzard 1975). It is interesting to note that such comparable results may reflect the similarity of some of the learning techniques used in SIMIG to those used by Blunt (1979), viz. discussion groups and complete statements of objectives. The delayed retention rates reported here are much better than those reported for medical anatomy by Sinclair (1965) and Shulman (1970): attrition rates were so marked (using responses from mcqs) that performance after one or two years was no better than might have been achieved by random guessing.

Although it was not possible to remove the effect of subsequent reinforcement (learning at a later time), a more rigorous estimate of attrition as loss may be provided by correcting overall performance data in Table 27

A   Numbers of students taking post-tests and delayed retention post-tests

Year	Post-test	+6 months	+12 months
1974	105	20	9
1975	101	32	56
1976	71	47	–
Totals	277	99	65

B   Performance on tests, expressed as overall performance (%) and corrected performance (%) ± SE with numbers of respondents in brackets.

	Post-test	+6 months	+12 months
Overall performance	75 ± 3	62 ± 4	51 ± 3
n.	(277)	(99)	(65)
Corrected performance	75 ± 3	53 ± 4	38 ± 4

C   Attrition rates as measured by percentage loss in performance from the post-test (rated as 100%) by two different (overall or corrected) indices ± SE with numbers of respondents in brackets.

Actual post-test	0-6 months	6-12 months	0-12 months
Overall	13 ± 7	11 ± 7	24 ± 6
Corrected	22 ± 7	15 ± 8	37 ± 7
n.	(99)	(39)	(65)
Post-test (as 100%)			
Overall	17 ± 9	15 ± 9	32 ± 8
Corrected	29 ± 9	20 ± 11	49 ± 8

Table 27
Attrition results.

for those items which students apparently 'learned' subsequent to the post-test. That is, by elimination of all response pairs except those correct in the first but incorrect in a subsequent test. This reduced the sample sizes as only sets of responses from the same student could be analysed. These results are expressed as 'corrected' (changes in) performance in Table 27. An example of the difference between this 'corrected' value for attrition with the interpretation as used by Blunt and Blizzard (1975) is: a student who loses three items that were originally correct and subsequently incorrect, but gains one item (originally incorrect and now correct), would have an attrition score of 1 minus 3 = −2 or −3 (corrected score). The values obtained for corrected rates of attrition are thus higher than by the other method of calculation, but represent the actual loss in performance.

Appendix C

Guidelines for Preparing Audio-visual Self-instructional Units

Audio-visual self-instructional units include tape-slides, audio-tutorial (A-T) units including modules (as in SIMIG), minicourses and other similar 'packages'.

All have features in common, but a tape-slide is a relatively simple production, whereas the others are more complex. This appendix includes:

1   Guidelines for making a tape-slide, with notes on the essential audio-visual equipment.
2   Guidelines for preparing a module (A-T unit).
3   Problems and pitfalls in A-T courses.

USING TAPE-SLIDES

A tape-slide is an audio-visual presentation in which a recorded audiotape is synchronized with the projection of relevant slide transparencies (35 mm). *Hardware* is the equipment which plays the tape and projects the slides. *Software* is the audiotape, slides, and any other material produced for use with the tape-slide, eg study guide notes, review questions.

Most tape-slide programmes are single concept units, used for self-instruction − in the cognitive or skills categories − and of 10 - 30 minutes duration.

Widely used in innovative teaching, tape-slide programmes are also useful additions to courses taught by traditional methods − where they may be viewed anywhere (library, laboratory) without the presence of a teacher.

A tape-slide may be used as:

a   The basic self-instructional unit, replacing a lecture.
b   Supplementary to material already presented by lecture or practical work.
c   Complementary material for general interest (maybe motivational), eg the SIMIG tape-slides on ecology and morphology, or complementary to the material presented in the carrel.
d   Summary or review programmes for self-evaluation, eg anatomy tape-slides in SIMIG.

For effective self-instruction as in (a) above, it is essential to plan for involvement of the learner and provide means for self-assessment. The steps in the preparation of the 'software' are set out below, and illustrated by a flow diagram (Fig. 23).

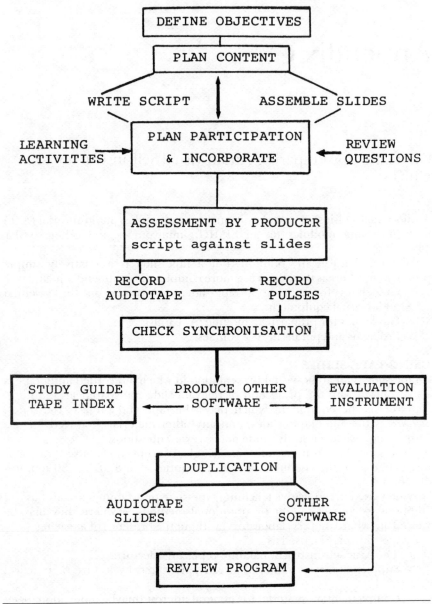

Figure 23
Flow diagram for preparation of a tape-slide.

PREPARING TAPE-SLIDES
1   Determine purpose of the programme; this is the instructional objective, reflected by the title of the tape-slide, eg 'How to make a tape-slide', 'How to use a pipette'.
2   Prepare a list of specific objectives, ie what the learner should be able to do on completion of the programme, and the desirable level of attainment.

3   Plan the overall content of the audiotape script to cover both objectives.
4   Write the first draft of the script (double-spaced to allow corrections) and note in the margin what slides will be required to illustrate each point. Some may be available already (eg used previously in lectures) and may even be the reason for making the presentation permanent.
5   Make a list of all the slides required, and arrange for the photography. Remember the golden rule — no slide is to remain on the screen when it ceases to be relevant! So, in addition to a title slide, you may have to use captions; a coloured blank is even preferable to an irrelevant slide. Make sure the detail or printing on any slide is legible to the viewer: a slide suitable for single viewing at close range may not be so for a larger audience (check on the projection screen to be used).
6   Plan learning activities at appropriate and convenient places in the script. These will vary according to the type of presentation. One of the simplest methods of participation is to request the viewer to hold the tape at 'pause', and answer questions posed by the audiotape, or printed in notes (eg study guide). The answer may then be given on tape when this is returned to 'play' mode, or supplied in the notes.
7   Assemble slides in sequence on a lightbox and examine the sequential order. It is more convenient to adjust changes in order on a lightbox than in a slide cartridge. If necessary make corresponding adjustments to the tape-script.
8   Arrange the slides in sequence in a slide cartridge. Project each one at the appropriate times as you read the draft of the script. Edit, using a conversational manner, while the slide is projected. At this stage one may discover that more captions are needed, ie necessary parts of the script are not relevant to the slide on the screen!
9   Type the final draft, and check that slide changes are clearly marked in the margin.
10 Record audiotape, reading from the script in a conversational tone. Ad-libbing usually results in redundancies. With some recorders, pulses have to be added at the same time, otherwise wait until (12).
11 Check the quality of the sound track by playback (recording at too high a level results in distortion).
12 Record pulses on audiotape for synchronization.
13´ Check synchronization.
14 Duplicate tape and reserve master tape for duplication only (tape may break if handled incorrectly). It is preferable to have a duplicate set of slides, but the master set may be used if security is adequate (cartridges can be sealed).
15 Produce other software, eg study guide or notes, tape index (all optional). Review questions should be available for self-assessment.
16 An evaluation instrument for students' comments provides feedback to the producer, useful in reviewing the programme.

AUDIO-VISUAL EQUIPMENT FOR TAPE-SLIDES
The hardware should be reliable and sturdy; recurring technical faults detract from any presentation. A cassette tape-recorder, a slide projector and a viewing screen are essential for tape-slides. These may be combined in a

portable unit resembling a small television set, but with an inbuilt cassette player and pulse translator. A circular slide cartridge may lock into the top of the unit or a straight cartridge may be inset at the base. One disadvantage is that audiotape and pulses cannot be recorded with this equipment, so an additional tape-recorder is required.

Some cassette tape-recorders have inbuilt pulse synchronizers. Alternatively these (small) units can be attached to the tape-recorder. The spoken word is recorded on one track of the tape, the electronic pulse on the other. The head in the tape-recorder translates the pulse through the appropriate track via the synchronizer to the projector for slide change. (Unfortunately several types of pulsing systems, usually incompatible, are in use. With some, audio and pulses may be recorded on both sides of the cassette tape, with others on one side only.)

The most sophisticated way of presenting tape-slides is by a dissolve unit linked to two or more projectors. The advantage is in the smooth transition from one image to another, eliminating an abrupt slide change.

For individual or dual viewing, rear screen projection is preferable (as in the compact portable units). The image is projected first onto a mirror and then reflected onto the back of the screen − ideal for daylight viewing.

In reviewing (by reversing) a tape-slide, there is one disadvantage: most machines do not reverse the slides automatically in conjunction with tape re-wind. But a tape index, showing the approximate position of each numbered slide on the tape counter, simplifies the procedure of finding, in review, the corresponding slide for a particular section of the commentary.

PREPARING A MODULE
Sufficient information has been given in the text (Chapter 2) to indicate what is involved in the production of a SIMIG module, or any audio-tutorial unit for self-instruction. The steps in preparing a unit, superficially similar to those for making a tape-slide, are briefly summarized:

1   List all the objectives (instructional and specific).
2   List all the media to be used in accomplishing the objectives (where carrels are equipped with projectors, 35 mm slide transparencies are frequently used).
3   List all the activities to be used for maximum involvement of the learner, inside and outside the carrel. These include reading printed material, following instructions in the study guide, actual specimens, demonstrations, quizzes for self-assessment − testing comprehension.
4   Assemble 2 and 3 in sequence.
5   Write the first draft of the script, incorporating 2 and 3.
6   Edit the script, using a conversational mode as if speaking to one student.
7   Optional − make a trial tape, then transcribe and re-edit (I find this wasteful in time).
8   Record the tape, reading from the script in a conversational tone. I use short musical interludes to indicate that the tape should be turned off (now) for self-quizzes or some other independent activity. These breaks may then be used for change of voice.
9   Duplicate tapes, retain master.

10 Produce and duplicate software (study guide, illustrations, photo-graphs, slides, etc.).

11 Evaluation instruments: one of the reasons why first 'trials' of A-T courses are rarely optimally effective, is that student feedback provides much of the information used in reviewing programmes. It is therefore useful to canvass opinions of each unit every week from both students and staff (especially demonstrators), and to use this information, together with students' 'end of course' responses to questionnaires (Chapter 8).

In the next section readers will discover that an effective A-T course also has a 'psychological substructure' not evident from the course outline or statements of objectives.

PROBLEMS AND PITFALLS IN AUDIO-TUTORIAL COURSES

'Problems and pitfalls in audio-tutorial methods' is the appropriate title for an Appendix in the book by Postlethwait et al. (1969) on the audio-tutorial (A-T) approach to learning. This is essential reference material for anyone venturing into the field of A-T instruction. The authors discuss problems and pitfalls under three headings:

1 Problems associated with structuring A-T
2 Problems associated with psychological issues
3 Technical deficiencies

The points covered in (1) but presented here in the positive mode are:

a Specification of instructional objectives (Mager 1962) is essential in the design of optimal instructional sequences, with an appropriate array of auditory, visual, printed and actual materials.

b Prior lecture notes are of limited use, because they do not incorporate simultaneous and direct experience with materials.

c Visuals should be chosen carefully to enhance learning. Too many or too complex visuals (photographs, diagrams) may confuse rather than clarify a concept.

d Use essential and appropriate study materials for clarifying concepts (ie exclude unnecessary materials).

e Auxiliary experiences in addition to carrel study provide a more effective A-T course, eg demonstrations, independent activities, discussions, frequent quiz sessions, or other evaluative feedback.

f In structuring A-T programmes, the design of sequential experiences in optimal order is of paramount importance. So also are optimal sequences of audio, visual or manipulatory experience, which can be identified by empirical testing.

In 'problems associated with psychological issues' (2) reference is made to the work of Bruner, Ausubel, Gagné and Skinner on learning theory and the critical importance that structure plays in instruction. Ausubel (1968) has formulated the most comprehensive description to guide planning of A-T instruction. His theory is that new learning proceeds only when the learner has the elemental concepts or 'subsumers' for assimilating new information. When these are lacking, new material should be introduced, with 'organiz-ers' (ie a more general statement or abstraction) and concrete experience with material.

Pacing and substructure are also important because learners have varying rates of assimilating new knowledge. Students with adequate subsuming concepts assimilate at a much faster rate than students who must rote-learn some information. 'Organizers' reduce rote learning, and for some, subsuming concepts will form only after sufficient knowledge has been acquired rotely. Provision of adequate time, in early instruction, for these inefficient learners is necessary to prevent rote learning of all subsequent related material (although rote learners may reproduce sufficient material at least to pass a course).

Tangible evidence of lack of subsuming concepts by the learners is provided when a lot of students report that they had to repeat a segment of an A-T course. From this feedback (common in first generation courses) the programmer can then provide the necessary 'organizers', and perhaps add more concrete material/examples. This is what the authors infer by psychological 'substructure'.

Small discussion sessions preferably with some structure and staff guidance, are some of the best methods for continuous monitoring of student feedback. This is useful not only for student self-assessment, but in the optimal design/reorganization of course structure. But emphasis should not be placed on small-step evaluation of learning; the objective is to produce learners with a hierarchical cognitive structure where small concepts are subsumed under larger ones to gain stability and permanence.

Students respond to affective factors as well as information-processing determinants. Students 'like' effective A-T instruction partly because of their awareness that they are learning meaningfully; positive motivation (cognitive drive) results from this awareness. Social motivation may be encouraged by planning segments where students can interact (for example in SIMIG groups), while independent problem-solving (in SIMIG groups and in the A-T project week) provides opportunities for independent discovery. Provision of coffee-tea facilities can have affective as well as cognitive pay-off.

In technical deficiencies (3) attention is drawn to cost-use matching, ie the unnecessary use of costly complex equipment when simple materials are just as effective. Examples given are the use of a movie film or videocassette when a tape-slide is adequate.

Abuses in quality of audio-visual materials are often found in A-T courses, by the use either of costly or of inexcusably poor materials.

Adequate space distribution in the learning centre means space for exhibits, demonstrations and experiments near the carrel units. An adjacent room(s) for reading, discussion and coffee-tea breaks is also highly desirable, although rarely available unless planned in new installations.

Associated systems such as accessible computer terminals are useful additions to some A-T courses. With large classes, the computer can be programmed for data processing, record keeping and testing by multiple choice questions.

References

Abercrombie, M. L. J. (1960) *The Anatomy of Judgement* London: Hutchinson; (1969) Harmondsworth: Penguin

Abercrombie, M. L. J. (1968) Learning to think in groups *Forum* 10 (3)

Abercrombie, M. L. J. (1970) *Aims and Techniques of Group Teaching* London: Society for Research into Higher Education (4th edition 1979) Guildford: Society for Research into Higher Education

Abercrombie, M. L. J. and Terry, P. M. (1978) *Talking to Learn: Improving Teaching and Learning in Small Groups* Guildford: Society for Research into Higher Education

Ashby, E. (1958) *Technology and the Academics* London: Macmillan

Ashby, E. (1974) *Adapting Universities to a Technological Society* London: Jossey Bass

Ausubel, D. P. (1968) *Educational Psychology; A cognitive view* New York: Holt, Rinehart and Winston

Bales, R. F. (1951) *Interaction Process Analysis* Cambridge, Mass.: Addison-Wesley

Barnett, S. A. (1958) An experiment with free discussion groups *Universities Quarterly* 12, 175-190

Beard, R. (1972) *Teaching and Learning in Higher Education* (2nd edition) Harmondsworth : Penguin

Block, J. H. (Ed.) (1971) *Mastery Learning: Theory and Practice* New York: Holt, Rinehart and Winston

Bloom, B. S. (Ed.) (1956) *Taxonomy of Educational Objectives: I Cognitive Domain* New York: David McKay

Bloom, B. S. (1968) *Learning for Mastery* UCLA-CSEIP Evaluation Comment 1, 2

Bloom, B. S. (1971) *Mastery Learning* In Block *op. cit.*

Bloom, B. S., Hastings, J. T. and Madaus, G. F. (1971) *Handbook on Formative and Summative Evaluation of Student Learning* McGraw Hill

Blunt, M. J. and Blizzard, P. J. (1975) Recall and retrieval of anatomical knowledge *British Journal of Medical Education* 9 (4) 255 - 63

Blunt, M. J. (1979) The use of educational groups in a basic medical science *Programmed Learning and Educational Technology* 16 (1) 57 - 69

Boreham, N. C. (1977) The effect of type of item on student-teacher interaction during feedback of examination performance *British Journal of Educational Psychology* 47, 335 - 338

Brewer, I. M. (1974) Recall, comprehension and problem-solving. Evaluation of an audiovisual method of learning plant anatomy *Journal of Biological Education* 8, 101 - 112

Brewer, I. M. (1977) SIMIG: A case study of an innovative method of teaching and learning *Studies in Higher Education* 2 (1) 33 - 54

Brewer, I. M. (1979) Group teaching strategies for promoting individual skills in problem solving *Programmed Learning and Educational Technology* 16 (2) 111 - 128

Brewer, I. M. and Tomlinson, J. D. (1981) SIMIG: The effect of time on performance with modular instruction *Programmed Learning and Educational Technology* 18 (2) 72 - 85

Brewer, I. M. and Tomlinson, J. D. (1981) The use of learning profiles in assessment and in the evaluation of teaching *Assessment and Evaluation in Higher Education* 6 (2) 120 - 164

Bruner, J. S. (1961) The act of discovery *Harvard Educational Review* 31, 11 - 32

Bruner, J. S. (1966) *Toward a Theory of Instruction* (7th printing 1975) Harvard University Press

Carroll, J. B. (1963) A model of school learning *Teachers College Record* 64, 723-33

Collier, K. G. (1980) Peer-group learning in higher education: the development of higher order skills *Studies in Higher Education* 5

Collier, K. G. (1983) *The Management of Peer-Group Learning. Syndicate Methods in Higher Education* Guildford: Society for Research into Higher Education

Comenius, J. A. (1896) *The Great Didactic* (Ed. M. W. Keatinge) London: Black

Fisher, K. M. and MacWhinney, B. (1976) AV Autotutorial instruction: a review of evaluative research *Audiovisual Communications Review* 24, 229 - 261

Gagné, R. M. and Rohwer, W. D. (1969) Instructional psychology *Annual Review of Psychology* 20, 381 - 418

Gephart, W. J. and Antonoplos, D. P. (1972) The effects of expectancy and other research biasing factors. In Sperry, L. (Ed.) *Learning Performance and Individual Differences, Essays and Readings* Illinois: Scott Foresman

Goldschmid, M. and Goldschmid, B. (1976) Peer teaching in higher education *Higher Education* 5

Hale Report (1964) Report of the Committee on *University Teaching Methods* (chairman, Sir Edward Hale) London: HMSO

Hamilton, D., Jenkins, D., King, C., MacDonald, B. and Parlett, M. (Eds) (1977) *Beyond the Numbers Game* London: MacMillan

Hurst, R. N. and Postlethwait, S. N. (1971) Minicourses at Purdue: an interim report. In Creager, J. G. and Murray, D. L. (Eds) *The Use of Modules in College Biology Teaching* Washington: Commission on Undergraduate Education in Biological Sciences

Johnson, M. L. (1950) Discussion methods in preclinical teaching *Lancet* 2, 313 - 17

Johnson, M. L. J. (1955) Observer error; its bearing on teaching *Lancet* 2, 422

Katzman, N. and Nyenhuis, J. (1972) Color vs. black-and-white: effects on learning, opinion and attention *Audiovisual Communications Review* 20, 16 - 30

Keller, F. S. (1968) Goodbye, Teacher *Journal of Applied Behavioural Analysis* 1, 79 - 89

Kelley, H. H. and Thibault, J. W. (1969) Group problem solving. In Lindzey, G. K. and Aronson, E. *Handbook of Social Psychology* (Volume IV) Reading, Mass: Addison-Wesley

La Gaipa, J. J. (1968) Programmed instruction, teacher ability and subject matter difficulty *Journal of Psychology* (Provincetown, Mass.) 68

McGuire, C. H. (1963) A process approach to the construction and analysis of medical examination *Journal of Medical Education* 38, 556

Mager, R. F. (1962) *Preparing Instructional Objectives* Palo Alto, California: Fearon

Markle, S. M. (1967) Empirical testing of programmes. In Lange, P. (Ed.) *Programmed Instruction* Chicago: University of Chicago Press

Marton, F. and Säljö, R. (1976 a) On qualitative differences in learning: I Outcome and process *British Journal of Educational Psychology* 46, 4 - 11

Marton, F. and Säljö, R. (1976 b) On qualitative differences in learning: II Outcome as a function of learner's conception of the task *British Journal of Educational Psychology* 46, 115 - 127

Owen, G. (1983) The tutor's role. In Collier, K. G. (Ed.) *op. cit.*

Parlett, M. and Hamilton, D. (1972) *Evaluation as Illumination: a new approach to the study of innovatory programmes* Edinburgh: Edinburgh University; published also in Hamilton, D. et al. (Eds) *op. cit.*

Parlett, M. and Dearden, G. (Eds) (1977) *Introduction to Illuminative Evaluation: Studies in Higher Education* California: Pacific Soundings Press

Postlethwait, S. N., Novak, J., and Murray, H. T., JR. (1969) *The Audio-tutorial Current Issues in Higher Education. Proc. 19th Annual National Conference on Higher Education* 134 - 135

Postlethwait, S. N., Novak, J., and Murray, H. T., JR. (1969) *The Audi-tutorial Approach to Learning* (3rd edition 1972) Minneapolis: Burgess

Postlethwait, S. N. and Russell, J. D. (1971) 'Minicourses' – The style of the future? In Creagor, J. G. and Murray, D. L. (Eds) *The Use of Modules in College Biology Teaching* Washington, DC: Commission on Undergraduate Education in the Biological Sciences

Potts, D. (1981) One-to-one learning. In Boud, D. (Ed.) *Developing Student Autonomy in Learning* London: Kogan Page

Rockford, K. J. (1975) Teaching, the heroic journey. In Buxton, T. H. and Pritchard, K. W. (Eds) *Excellence in University Teaching* South Carolina: University of South Carolina Press

Rudduck, J. (1978) *Learning Through Small Group Discussion. A Study of Seminar Work in Higher Education* Guildford: Society for Research into Higher Education

Schulman, L. J. (1970) Report to the faculty: office of research in medical education, University of Illinois College of Medicine. Cited in Schulman, Lee. G. *Journal of Medical Education* 45, 90 - 100

Sinclair, D. (1965) An experiment in the teaching of anatomy *British Journal of Medical Education* 40, 401 - 413

Steffen, R. F. (1972) Unobtrusive observation of student non-verbal behaviour in audio-tutorial self-instruction (Doctoral dissertation, Syracuse University, 1971) *Dissertation Abstracts International* 32, 5678A - 5679A (University Microfilms No. 72 - 11,876)

Witkin, H. A. et al. (1977) Field-dependent and field-independent cognitive styles and their educational implications *Review of Educational Research* 47, 1 - 64

Index